**Books are to be returned on or before
the last date below.**

26. JUN. 2008		

LIBREX —

D0541332

Robert Ingram / Paul Duncan (Ed.)

FRANÇOIS TRUFFAUT

Film Author 1932–1984

TASCHEN

KÖLN LONDON LOS ANGELES MADRID PARIS TOKYO

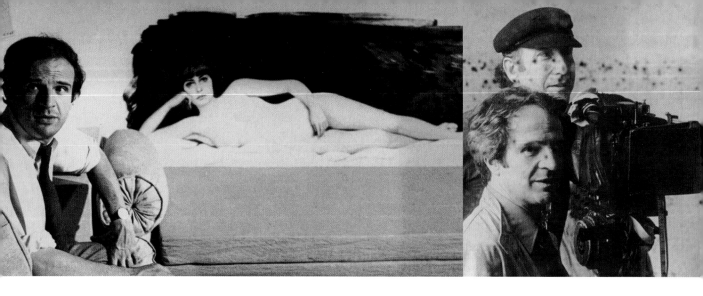

FRONT COVER
Still from 'Le Dernier Métro' (1980)

FIRST PAGE
On the set of 'L'Amour en fuite' (1979)
François Truffaut and Jean-Pierre Léaud created and developed the character of Antoine Doinel over 20 years.

FRONTISPIECE
On the set of 'Fahrenheit 451' (1966)
On the one hand Truffaut loved reading and was thrilled when he had his first book published. But he also liked to make little fires in ashtrays. Truffaut battles with both of these conflicting desires in 'Fahrenheit 451.'

THIS PAGE
1 On the set of 'La Mariée était en noir' (1967) Truffaut in front of a painting of Jeanne Moreau.
2 On the set of 'L'Amour en fuite' (1979) Cinematographer Nestor Almendros (background) worked on eight films with Truffaut.

To stay informed about upcoming TASCHEN titles, please request our magazine at www.taschen.com or write to TASCHEN America, 6671 Sunset Boulevard, Suite 1508, USA-Los Angeles, CA 90028, Fax: +1-323-463.4442.
We will be happy to send you a free copy of our magazine which is filled with information about all of our books.

© 2004 TASCHEN GmbH
Hohenzollernring 53, D–50672 Köln
www.taschen.com

OPPOSITE
On the set of 'La Nuit américaine' (1973)

PAGES 6/7
On the set of 'Fahrenheit 451' (1966)
François Truffaut (right) with his interpreter and friend Helen G. Scott and cinematographer Nic Roeg (left).

BACK COVER
On the set of 'Fahrenheit 451' (1966)
François Truffaut.

Editor/Layout:
Paul Duncan/Wordsmith Solutions

Editorial Coordination:
Thierry Nebois, Cologne

Typeface Design:
Sense/Net, Andy Disl, Cologne

Printed in Italy
ISBN 3–8228–2260–4

Notes
A superscript number indicates a reference to a note on page 192

Thanks
To François Truffaut's children (Laura, Eva and Joséphine) for their permission and suggestions. To Madeleine Morgenstern, Robert Lachenay and Raymond Cauchetier for their pictures and stories. And to Nathaneal Karmitz and Monique Holveck at MK2.

Image Sources
MK2, Paris: 1, 8, 10 (3), 11, 12/13, 15, 16 (2), 19, 22 (8), 23 (3), 41, 46, 47, 48 (2), 56, 58, 60, 62, 63, 67, 69 (2), 75, 88, 89, 90, 91, 92, 93 (2), 94, 95 (2), 96, 97, 99 (2), 110, 111 (2), 112/113, 113 (2), 114 (2), 115 (2), 116, 117, 118/119, 119, 120/121, 122, 124, 127, 128/129, 136, 137, 138/139, 140, 142 (2), 143 (3), 144 (2), 148, 150/151, 151, 152/153, 154 (2), 155, 157, 159, 160/161, 162, 163 (3), 165, 170/171, 172, 173, 175, 179, 180, 181
British Film Institute Stills, Posters and Designs, London: 2, 4 (2), 6/7, 11 (2), 14, 19, 20 (2), 23 (3), 39 (2), 40, 41, 42, 43, 44, 49, 54, 58/59, 61, 62, 63, 74, 76, 77, 81 (2), 82/83, 89, 96, 97, 104, 105, 108, 132, 133, 134, 135, 147, 156, 165, 168, 185, Back Cover
BiFi, Paris: 5, 16, 20, 21, 22, 23 (3), 38, 40, 52, 53, 57, 68, 101, 124, 125, 126 (2), 130/131, 141, 168, 171 (2), 174, 176.
PWE Verlag / defd-movies, Hamburg: Front Cover, 18, 22 (2), 23, 32, 33, 53 (2), 78/79, 80 (2), 81, 86 (2), 87 (2), 90, 104, 155, 158, 166, 167, 169, 177, 179, 182/183
Robert Lachenay Collection, France: 29, 30, 31 (3), 34, 34/35, 36, 37 (2), 185 (2)
Raymond Cauchetier: 55, 64, 65, 66, 70, 71, 72
Joel Finler: 15, 22, 23, 50, 102, 105, 178
Family Truffaut Collection, Paris: 24, 26, 27, 28, 29 (2), 184
Raymond Depardon/Magnum/Ag. Focus: 106, 107, 123
Corbis: 84 (Sunset Boulevard/Corbis Sygma)
The Kobal Collection, London/New York: 146, 147
Photofest, New York: 80, 134
Cahiers du cinéma: 23 (Coll. cdc/D. Rabourdin)
Jean Marquis: 100

Image Copyrights
The film images in this book are copyright to the respective photographers: Robert Lachenay (Les Mistons, Tirez sur le pianiste), André Dino/MK2 (Les Quatre Cents Coups), Raymond Cauchetier (Tirez sur le pianiste, Jules et Jim, Antoine et Colette, La Peau douce, Baisers volés), Norman Hargood (Fahrenheit 451), Marilu Parolini (La Mariée était en noir), Léonard De Raemy (La Sirène du Mississippi), Pierre Zucca (L'Enfant sauvage, Domicile conjugal, Les Deux Anglaises et le Continent, Une belle fille comme moi, La Nuit américaine), Bernard Prim (L'Histoire d'Adèle H.), Hélène Jeanbreau (L'Argent de poche), Mme Dominique Le Rigoleur (L'Homme qui aimait les femmes, La Chambre verte, L'Amour en fuite), Jean-Pierre Fizet (Le Dernier Métro), Alain Venisse (La Femme d'à côté, Vivement dimanche!).
We deeply regret it if, despite our concerted efforts, any copyright owners have been unintentionally overlooked and omitted. Obviously we will amend any such errors in the next edition if they are brought to the attention of the publisher.

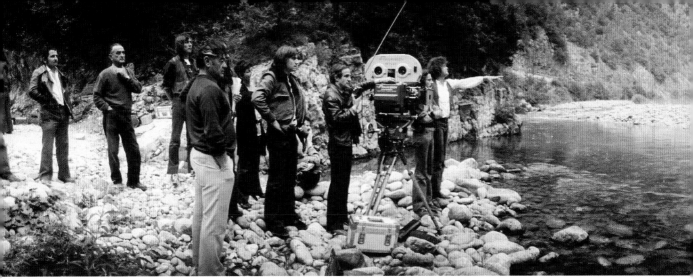

CONTENTS

TIREZ SUR LE PIANISTE
REALISATEUR : F. TRUFFAUT .
OPERATEUR : R. COUTARD .
N° 39/3A
Pse 2
NUIT
SONORE

Prelude

'I am a being of dialogue, everything in me is conflict and contradiction. However great the concern for truth, memoirs are never more than half true: everything is always more complicated than you think. Perhaps you can get closer to the truth in a novel.'[1]

With these words, the twentieth-century French writer André Gide concisely summarised the dilemma facing autobiographers. Fiction does not bind and restrict in the ways that autobiography does. Authors are more likely to be able to capture the truth if not shackled by an obligation to reality. Truffaut arrived at this conclusion early in his career.

Details of his personal life, even intimate ones, feed into his films: sometimes directly, e.g. the fictional Antoine Doinel taking a flat opposite Colette's in *Antoine et Colette* reflected François moving in opposite Liliane Litvin, and the stark "It's my mother sir, she's dead" is the excuse for truancy used by Antoine in *Les Quatre Cents Coups* and by Truffaut in his childhood. On other occasions, the event is transformed in its passage into film. Thus Antoine meets Colette at a concert whereas François met Liliane at the *Cinémathèque*. The overriding concern was the appropriateness and resonance of the event in the narrative. Thus, 'aspects of Truffaut's... childhood and adolescence enter his films not at the level of narrative detail, but at that of underlying structures and themes, the significance of which goes well beyond the personal.'[2]

It is not solely in the films such as those in the Doinel cycle or *La Nuit américaine* that autobiographical detail provides material. As Suzanne Schiffman wrote, 'I always had the impression, and he said this himself, that Truffaut said as much about himself in his adaptations as he did in his original scenarios.'[3] A film such as *Jules et Jim*, adapted from a novel by Henri-Pierre Roché, is just as revealing of Truffaut as a Doinel film. Roché's novel had attracted the director's interest because its author's life echoed aspects of Truffaut's. The latter took from the novel those experiences, characters, ideas and attitudes that resonated with his own. Thus, novel and film share common themes: the viability of the couple and alternative ways of living, the nature of desire, sexuality, friendship, the sheer pleasure of telling stories and the ways in which they can be told.

"Ideas are less interesting than the human beings who have them."

François Truffaut [4]

"It's better if children are badly brought up and happy than well brought up and unhappy."

François Truffaut [5]

TOP
Still from 'Les Quatre Cents Coups' (1959)
Throughout his career, Truffaut depicted the lives of children, perhaps because of his own childhood experiences. Here Antoine Doinel (Jean-Pierre Léaud) steals some milk to drink when he spends the night away from home.

RIGHT
Still from 'L'Enfant sauvage' (1969)
When we first see Victor (Jean-Pierre Cargol) living in the forest, he is an animal who forages for food.

BOTTOM
On the set of 'L'Argent de poche' (1976)
François Truffaut coaches Sylvie Grézel on the use of a megaphone. Her character is so hard-headed that she is left alone in her apartment instead of going to Sunday lunch. Hungry, she appeals to the neighbours for food. This is based on a true story told to Truffaut by Madeleine Morgenstern.

Other images of Truffaut's interaction with children can be seen on pages 46, 47, 95, 106, 107, 142 & 144.

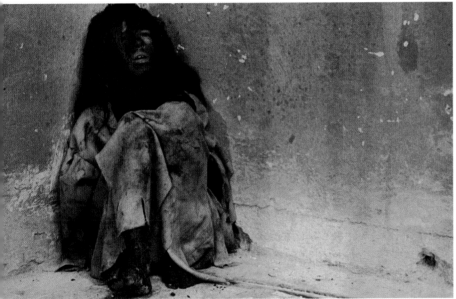

TOP
Still from 'Les Quatre Cents Coups' (1959)
After stealing a typewriter from his stepfather's
workplace, Antoine spends the night in jail.

LEFT
Still from 'L'Enfant sauvage' (1969)
The wild child, Victor, is captured and held in
Rodez police station.

BOTTOM
Still from 'L'Argent de poche' (1976)
Julien Leclou (Philippe Goldmann) is thrown out
of his home and spends the night on the streets.
It later transpires that his mother beats him
regularly and that he has bruises, scars and
burns all over his body.

On the set of 'L'Enfant sauvage' (1969)
François Truffaut plays Dr Itard, who teaches
Victor how to become civilised. However, in
doing so, he strips Victor of the senses he needs
to survive in the wild, effectively trapping Victor
in a world where he is unhappy.

Still from 'Les Quatre Cents Coups' (1959)
Truffaut's admiration of the female form is
evident in all his films. Here Antoine Doinel's
mother (Claire Maurier) is welcomed home by
his stepfather (Albert Rémy).

Other examples of the female form in Truffaut's
films can be seen on pages 33, 53, 76, 96, 110,
113, 116, 124, 125, 150/151, 152/153, 168 &
172.

*"You have with women the same relationship you
had with your mother."*

François Truffaut [6]

But his life was far from being the only source of ideas, characters and dialogue.
These were just as likely to come from newspapers, friends' anecdotes, books he
read and films he saw. Everything was grist to the mill, and little was sacrosanct, to
the occasional irritation of those around him.

In a directorial career spanning 29 years from 1954 to 1983, Truffaut made a
remarkable 24 films, three of which were shorts and 21 of which were full-length
feature films. Commentators have often remarked on the way in which the films of
Truffaut form an inseparable, overlapping whole. Structural, thematic and formal
aspects are echoed and contrasted from film to film. To get an overview of the
nature and extent of his work, it is useful to categorise his films.

A first group of films stands out immediately: the five that recount the
childhood, adolescence and early adult life of Antoine Doinel. These are *Les Quatre
Cents Coups* (1959), *Antoine et Colette* (1962), *Baisers volés* (1968), *Domicile
conjugal* (1970) and *L'Amour en fuite* (1979). Secondly come those that can be
loosely described as genre films. Most obviously attributable to this category is the
science-fiction film *Fahrenheit 451* (1966), though here as elsewhere the science-
fiction elements provide a vehicle for Truffaut's familiar concerns. Other 'genre' films
are more difficult to classify. *Tirez sur le pianiste* (1960), *La Mariée était en noir* (1967)
and *Vivement dimanche!* (1983) owe much to the American thrillers that spawned

Still from 'La Femme d'à côté' (1981)
In a lighthearted moment, Mathilde Bauchard
(Fanny Ardant, right) finds herself suddenly
disrobed when her dress catches on a chair.

Still from 'L'Homme qui aimait les femmes' (1977)
When Bertrand Morane looks in the window of a
lingerie shop, he sees Hélène (Geneviève
Fontanel). She goes out on a date with Morane,
but tells him that she prefers younger men,
which prompts Morane to write his memoirs.

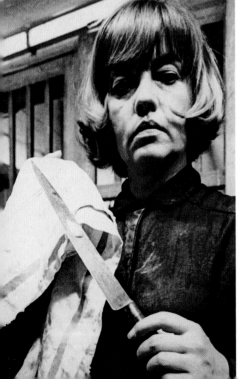

them. However, the difficulty of classification is highlighted by the fact that *Tirez sur le pianiste* has elements of several other genres while *Vivement dimanche!* is, in part at least, a Hollywood-style romantic comedy. *La Peau douce* (1964), *La Sirène du Mississippi* (1969) and *La Femme d'à côté* (1981) are similarly regarded primarily – but not exclusively – as 'films noirs.' Another cluster of films can be grouped together on the basis that they are 'historical.' This group includes *Jules et Jim* (1962), *L'Enfant sauvage* (1969), *Les Deux Anglaises et le Continent* (1971), *L'Histoire d'Adèle H.* (1975), *La Chambre verte* (1978) and *Le Dernier Métro* (1980). Again, however, this classification can only be superficial.

Those who create draw on the works of others to a greater or lesser extent. Truffaut was no exception and freely acknowledged his debts to writers and directors alike. The important and contrasting influences of directors Alfred Hitchcock and Jean Renoir have been the subject of detailed analyses, most significantly by Annette Insdorf.[7] Roberto Rossellini, Ernst Lubitsch and Howard Hawks are only a few of many directors whose films Truffaut knew intimately, sequence by sequence in many cases. At the same time, he read extensively and with a healthy eclecticism, books ranging from the classics of Honoré de Balzac, Marcel Proust and Jean Genet to the thrillers of American writers such as David Goodis, William Irish/Cornell Woolrich and Charles Williams. And of course, any book dealing with virtually any aspect of cinema. Jean Cocteau and Sacha Guitry – writers who also made films – provided role models for Truffaut.

He wanted to be a writer almost as much as he wanted to make films and his first creative pieces were a film scenario and two short stories, though nothing came of these.

Truffaut's films are, however, only part of his contribution to cinema. His role as film critic in the 1950s is arguably just as significant. His acerbic assaults on numerous French directors of the day, together with his enthusiastic promotion of directors from the Golden Age of French cinema and from the United States, led directly to a new type of film and new ways of making them. This was the New Wave, launched in 1959 with a spate of French films made in a new mould. Inasmuch as there was theory underpinning the new movement, Truffaut again contributed significantly by introducing, after Alexandre Astruc and his 'caméra-stylo' (camera-pen), the concept of the 'auteur,' the film-maker as author.

As a person, Truffaut presented a complex and often contradictory face to the world. He was highly intelligent, but almost entirely self-taught. He had strongly held beliefs but was apolitical. He defended his privacy fiercely – mostly by strict compartmentalisation of his life – but became a widely known public figure. Many have commented on his shyness – a trait reflected in several characters in his films. He retained the formal address with colleagues and even friends. Suzanne Schiffman reports that for Truffaut, 'three was a crowd.'[8] Despite this reserve and reluctance to join groups, he had an enormous circle of friends and acquaintances. And he was loyal, keeping in touch usually by letter. Yet without asking, he sold books belonging to his closest childhood friend, Robert Lachenay. To numerous critics, he was a misogynist, but he often made films with strong female characters. Josianne Couëdel, his secretary at the Films du Carrosse (the film company he created in 1957), recalled how he 'sought to push me forward, to give me confidence, to help me lose my shyness.'[9] In a similar vein, he was renowned for the tact and consideration he showed towards those who acted in his films. Others report that he was autocratic and unhelpful.

OPPOSITE TOP
On the set of 'Vivement dimanche!' (1983)
Men get mad but women get even. There are several femmes fatales in Truffaut's films. Here Fanny Ardant holds a gun on Truffaut.

OPPOSITE BOTTOM LEFT
Publicity still for 'La Mariée était en noir' (1967)
Julie Kohler (Jeanne Moreau) holds the knife that will kill her fifth victim. She has already pushed, poisoned and shot (with bullet and arrow) her previous victims.

OPPOSITE BOTTOM RIGHT
Still from 'L'Homme qui aimait les femmes' (1977)
Bertrand Morane (Charles Denner) is fascinated by Delphine Grezel (Nelly Borgeaud) who likes to make love in public places because it excites her. Her unhinged personality will lead to the shooting of her husband.

Other femmes fatales can be seen on pages 77, 127 & 177.

One area in which he remained unchanged throughout his adolescent and adult life was in his attraction to the opposite sex. Truffaut was the model for Bertrand Morane (*L'Homme qui aimait les femmes*) and Charles Denner played Bertrand as Truffaut, or at least (re)presenting a facet of Truffaut's make-up. From the numerous women he knew around the time of Liliane Litvin through to Fanny Ardant, he had a string of relationships – some of them with France's most talented actresses: Jeanne Moreau, Claude Jade, Françoise Dorléac, Jacqueline Bisset, Leslie Caron, Catherine Deneuve, Fanny Ardant. And we must not overlook the beautiful and gifted Madeleine Morgenstern, wife and friend from 1956. A remarkable aspect of these relationships is that when they ended, the friendship survived, strongly. As de Baecque and Toubiana pointed out in their richly detailed biography, 'Unfaithful, François Truffaut was always that, but more from a need to seduce and be loved than from a desire to emulate Don Juan.'[11] In simple terms, he spent his life seeking the love his mother denied him, desperate to prove himself worthy of love, over and over again.

A few quick brush-strokes will help to give an idea of Truffaut in his day-to-day routine. To paraphrase Molière, he ate to live rather than lived to eat. Eating out was rarely a pleasure: a working lunch with a sandwich was his normal fare. He loved and was proud of his old IBM typewriter on which he wrote most of his scenarios. Josianne Couëdel notes his love of TV and popular culture, his fascination with soaps such as *Dallas*. He knew the songs of many French singers by heart, e.g. Boby Lapointe, Charles Aznavour, Félix Leclerc, Charles Trenet, and used them in his films.[12] Above all, he loved going to the cinema. He would take his favourite 16mm films with him on shoots for the crew and cast's entertainment in the evenings. This passion for cinema, it might be argued, is linked to his unhappy childhood. From an early age he sought refuge, literally, in the cinema. For Truffaut, as for Ferrand in *La Nuit américaine*, it was a case of '[Letting] cinema reign!' For Truffaut, cinema was life.

There can be little doubt that Truffaut was less interested in ideas than in the people who have them. At the heart of every one of his films are the characters, their feelings, their relationships. Truffaut is not generally seeking to explore philosophical, political, religious or any other form of truth. While his films, with his writings, reveal a highly intelligent and creative mind, they cannot usually be described as intellectual, in comparison, say, to the films of Jean-Luc Godard, Alain Resnais or Eric Rohmer. The main themes of his work include 'childhood, male fascination with women, construction of masculinity, the obsession with death, the fumbling towards an understanding of love, the relationship of the individual with authority, the links between fiction and reality.'[13] To these can be added the act of creation – films, books, plays, paintings or cartoons – and the tensions arising from the conflict between that which is provisional and that which is absolute, permanent, definitive. Truffaut's concern with form is so predominant that it too might be considered a theme. Thus, narrative structure(s) and how to tell stories in the medium of film are important components of all the films.

The films are characterised by a mixture of elation and melancholy, often reflected in their music. Truffaut chooses songs or scores that comprise both elements and that slip from one mood to the other. The music accompanying *Les Mistons* is an excellent example. Another important feature is humour. Often producing a wry and nuanced smile rather than a belly laugh, it acts as

Still from 'Les Deux Anglaises et le Continent' (1971)
Many of Truffaut's films feature funerals, graveyards and the death of the central characters. For example, Gérard dies in 'Les Mistons', Léna in 'Tirez sur le pianiste', Catherine and Jim in 'Jules et Jim', Pierre Lachenay in 'La Peau douce', Anne Brown in 'Les Deux Anglaises et le Continent', Bertrand Morane in 'L'Homme qui aimait les femmes', Julien Davenne in 'La Chambre verte' and Bernard and Mathilde in 'La Femme d'à côté'. Above, Claude Roc (Jean-Pierre Léaud) mourns the death of his mother.

For more examples of death see images on pages 50, 84, 86, 95, 97, 156-159 & 180.

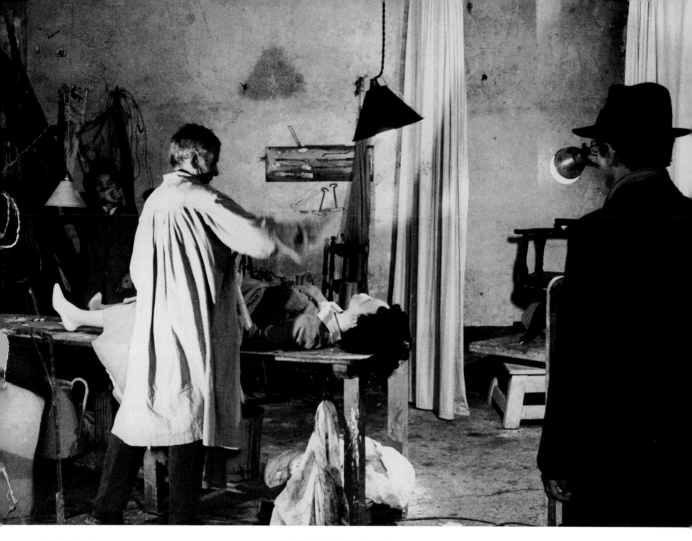

ABOVE
Still from 'La Chambre verte' (1978)
Julien Davenne (François Truffaut, right) orders
the life-size waxwork figure of his dead wife to
be destroyed.

LEFT
Still from 'Jules et Jim' (1962)
Jules (Oskar Werner, right) follows the remains of
the two people he loved, Catherine and Jim.

counterpoint to the sadder, more reflective moments. Thus *Les Quatre Cents Coups* frequently makes us smile while simultaneously presenting the unhappiness of a neglected, wilful child. Elation, melancholy, humour then, but rarely violence. As Truffaut explained, 'Like me, Antoine is against violence because it means confrontation. What replaces violence is running away, not to avoid what is essential but to obtain it.'[14]

'The true director does not toy with the spectator: rather he colludes with him.'[15] Jean Gruault here evokes a key trait of Truffaut's style. The latter often hankered after the days of silent films, regretting the 'secret' that had been lost with the advent of sound. This 'secret' (which became the title of Anne Gillain's book on Truffaut, *The Lost Secret*) alluded to the viewers' alert participation in the creation of meaning, i.e. to 'interpret what they saw, to solve the riddle posed knowingly and constantly by young (and some less young) film-makers who for the most part had learned their trade or made their career in silent films.'[16] Truffaut's style is self-reflective, comprising a profusion of nods and winks to his viewers, e.g. the homage to Abel Gance in the tripartite image/screen featuring Plyne in *Tirez sur le pianiste* and to Jean Renoir in the use of a courtyard set for *Domicile conjugal*. He did not, however, prompt a re-evaluation of form, as did Godard. Rather, Truffaut was a master of the art of film-making, having learned his trade in the cinemas of Paris through the thousands of films he saw from the age of eight onwards. And about which he made extensive notes, filed away in his famous 'dossiers.'

Truffaut was, then, a director who dealt in emotions but who saw intellectualism almost as a defect,[17] who used the full range of film techniques to great effect but who was rarely innovative, who at times appears grossly misogynist and politically incorrect. Where does he stand today? Can he be classed as a great director? One answer is provided by Helen Scott, Truffaut's American friend and co-author of *Hitchcock/Truffaut* (Ramsay, 1983). In her contribution to *Le Roman de François Truffaut* she writes, 'I don't know if François Truffaut was the best director in the world but in his humanity, his statements and his writings and to judge by the enormous number of letters he received from the farthest corners of the USA, from Scandinavia, from Japan and elsewhere, I believe he was the world's most widely respected and most widely loved.'[18]

Truffaut's films had a wide audience, both in France and abroad. They stimulate reflection in areas affecting us all. If this reflection focuses primarily on our emotional rather than intellectual lives and leads to a better understanding of ourselves and how we relate to others, it is no less important for that. As Georges Kiejman, Truffaut's lawyer, put it, 'François did not make social films, films with a message. But, describing the happiness of individuals, is that not in itself equivalent to adopting a political stance?'[19] Truffaut's success stems from his films simultaneously appealing to French and international audiences. His films deal with emotions that provide a terrain familiar to everyone, wherever they live, whatever language they speak.

ABOVE
Still from 'L'Homme qui aimait les femmes' (1977)
Truffaut's love of books is evident in virtually all his films. Here editor Geneviève Bigey (Brigitte Fossey) presents Bertrand Morane (Charles Denner) with a dummy of his book.

OPPOSITE TOP
Still from 'Fahrenheit 451' (1966)

OPPOSITE BOTTOM LEFT
Still from 'Baisers volés' (1968)
Antoine Doinel (Jean-Pierre Léaud) reads Honoré de Balzac's 'The Lily in the Valley.'

OPPOSITE BOTTOM RIGHT
Still from 'Tire-au-flanc' (1962)
Truffaut is reading the economical Fayard edition of Goethe's 'Werther' in Claude de Givray's film, which Truffaut produced.

Other book-orientated images can be seen on pages 80, 81, 155, 163 & 166.

Visual Motifs

Fire

Truffaut had the habit of lighting matches in ashtrays, so it is no surprise that many of his films feature unexpected fires. Shown are 'Les Quatre Cents Coups,' 'Domicile conjugal,' 'La Chambre verte' and 'La Femme d'à côté.' Further images are on pages 2, 80–83, 105, 158 & 159.

Caresses

Caressing the face, usually framed in profile, is a prelude to a kiss. Shown are 'La Peau douce,' 'Baisers volés,' 'L'Histoire d'Adèle H.' and 'L'Amour en fuite.' Further images are on pages 117 & 167.

Slaps

Like fire, the slap is sudden and unexpected. Shown are 'Les Quatre Cents Coups,' 'Jules et Jim,' 'La Peau douce' and 'La Femme d'à côté.' Further images are on pages 61 & 175. (Note that the still for 'Les Quatre Cents Coups' is incorrectly posed because Antoine is asked which hand he would like and he selects the left hand.)

Windows

Truffaut's characters often look through windows, communicate through them, or are filmed through them. Shown are 'La Peau douce,' 'La Chambre verte,' 'L'Amour en fuite' and 'Vivement dimanche!' Further images are on pages 10, 41, 64, 86, 102, 135, 142, 143, 144, 149 & 150.

Cinema

It is no surprise that a passionate lover of film like Truffaut would include numerous references to the cinema in his own films. Shown are 'Les Quatre Cents Coups,' 'Jules et Jim,' 'Domicile conjugal' and 'L'Argent de poche.' Further images are on pages 43, 75, 130–131 & 134.

Positioning

Some of Truffaut's characters arrange the position of other characters. Obviously, Truffaut did this to his actors but it is curious that the action is included in his films. Shown are 'La Mariée était en noir,' 'L'Enfant sauvage,' 'Les Deux Anglaises et le Continent' and 'La Nuit américaine.' Further images are on pages 105 & 127.

Father Unknown
1932–1959

Early in the morning of 6 February 1932, discreetly, some distance from her family home in Paris' 9th *arrondissement* and on her own, Janine de Monferrand gave birth to a boy. Janine was 19 and the daughter of respectable middle-class parents. An unmarried mother was a source of shame in such circles and the child, christened François, was placed in the care of a wet-nurse. Eighteen months later, on marrying Janine, Roland Truffaut, architectural draughtsman, accepted the fatherless boy and gave him a surname.

Roland Truffaut's great passion was mountaineering. Janine was more interested in books, the theatre, cinema and romance. François was not allowed to disrupt their life and until the age of 10 was brought up mainly by his maternal grandmother. On her death, it was his stepfather who argued for his return to the family home. François' attitude to his mother (and vice versa) was complicated: he admired her beauty and independent spirit but continually felt he was in the way. 'What shall we do with the kid?' was a constant refrain and his parents repeatedly left him alone at weekends, and even at Christmas.[21] It did not take him long to discover the truth about his origins, and his sense of his mother's resentment towards him intensified. He sought company elsewhere and found it in Robert Lachenay, a lifelong friend who, as the character René, features in *Les Quatre Cents Coups* and *Antoine et Colette*. The young Truffaut spent much of his time with Robert, often staying overnight at his flat.

After encouraging reports in his early school days, his school life became difficult as he attended a number of different institutions, where his lack of success was matched only by his increased truancy. The famous sequence from *Les Quatre Cents Coups* in which he explains one of his absences to the teacher by blurting, 'My mother died' is taken from his life. There could be no more poignant statement of what was, to the young boy, a psychological 'truth.' Truancy and running away from home were the beginning of a slide into petty crime. The theft of a typewriter, documented in *Les Quatre Cents Coups,* to pay off debts accruing from his ill-fated attempts to run a film club, Le Cercle Cinémane, brought him to the attention of the police. Rescued once by an ashamed Roland Truffaut, it was the latter who, exasperated by his son's recidivist behaviour, delivered François himself to the police, leading to internment at a detention centre. At about this time, Truffaut came into contact with André Bazin, an eminent film critic, who offered him work with the organisation 'Travail et Culture.'

François Truffaut, aged 10 (1942)
Truffaut had a lifelong passion for reading, and this was evident in the subjects he filmed (often based on books). Many of his film characters also read or write books (see pages 20 & 21).

"My mother just could not stand noise, or rather I ought to say, to be more accurate, that she could not stand me. Anyway, I had to pretend I wasn't there and sit on a chair reading. I was not allowed to play or make any noise. I had to make people forget I existed."

François Truffaut [22]

This was the first of several short-lived jobs before his impetuous decision to join the army at the end of 1950. Within days he was regretting his decision. There followed a wretched period including an attempted suicide, bouts of syphilis and desertion before he was officially discharged early in 1952. The Bazins had played a role in his release and for the next two years Truffaut lived with them in their home at Bry-sur-Marne.

From the age of eight, Truffaut became a regular cinema-goer: between 1946 and 1956 it is said he watched more than 3000 films, often as many as three a day. Initially, these were mostly French and German – but increasingly, after the cessation of hostilities, they were American as well. At the same time he had inherited the reading habit of his mother and grandmother and was getting through three books a week, often thrillers. His 'addiction' to film began in the war years. With their warmth and darkness, the cinemas of Paris offered a refuge. His visits were clandestine (he did not tell his parents) and illegal (he entered via the exit). The strength of his passion for film is reflected in the files that he began to keep on directors and films. But seeing films was not enough; he had to talk about them. Regular visits to the Cinémathèque were supplemented with attendance at a variety of film clubs. It was at the Cinémathèque that he met Godard, Rohmer, Claude Chabrol, Jacques Rivette, Doniol-Valcroze and Liliane Litvin, his first serious girlfriend and the model for Colette in *Antoine et Colette*. Bazin encouraged him to write and his first articles appeared in the spring of 1950. This was the beginning of a meteoric rise to prominence as a film critic: he made over 500 contributions to the right-wing *Arts* and nearly 200 to *Cahiers du cinéma*, among the most influential film journals of the day. Bazin also organised and funded trips to film festivals.

Truffaut's writing on film is characterised by its forthright and highly focused style. The style of criticism in the 1950s, when he did most of his work, was superseded by the more intellectual and theoretical approach that has dominated since. Truffaut's views were shaped by a sharp sense of what he believed was wrong with French cinema and by his encyclopaedic knowledge of European and American cinema. He attacked directors he disliked and promoted those he favoured. Cumulatively, his reviews came to define 'bad' films and directors and, conversely, those that were influential. There was, however, little sustained theoretical underpinning.

One article sums up Truffaut's style and his views on French cinema. 'A Certain Tendency in French Cinema' was the product of over two years' work in which, with help from Bazin, he wrote what was to be his single most important statement on cinema. It was published in the *Cahiers du cinéma* in January 1954 and had an immediate and widespread impact. The targets of Truffaut's criticisms were the most widely known French directors of the day. Among the most significant and bearing the brunt of his assault were Claude Autant-Lara, Jean Delannoy, René Clément and Yves Allégret. And even more to blame than the directors were the scriptwriters and, in particular, Jean Aurenche and Pierre Bost. They were the ones principally responsible for what Truffaut labelled the 'tradition of quality' and the vogue for psychological realism. He accuses them of being anti-clerical, blasphemous, sarcastic and bent on deceiving their public. Their films were, he opined, artificial and unnatural, and marred by 'literary' dialogue, an overuse of studio sets and excessively polished photography. Their psychological realism was, Truffaut bluntly declared, neither real nor psychological.

ABOVE
François Truffaut (circa 1934)

OPPOSITE
François Truffaut (circa 1939)
François lived with his maternal grandmother in Paris, but during the summer they moved to Binic in Brittany, where he enjoyed reading, walks and running wild on the beach. The hair suggests Victor in 'L'Enfant sauvage' and Julien Leclou in 'L'Argent de poche'.

Truffaut attacked the notion that scriptwriters are the real authors of a film. This was anathema to him and led directly to one of the central tenets of the New Wave, *la politique des auteurs* or 'author theory.' 'I cannot believe in the peaceful co-existence of the Tradition of Quality and a cinema of authors,' wrote Truffaut in his article.[23] The somewhat crude 'author theory' seeks to equate the director of a film with the author of a book or play. This 'equation' can only be an approximation since any film is inevitably the outcome of work by a team of people, including the director, scriptwriter(s), actors, cinematographer, technicians and above all editors. Truffaut often worked closely with the editor – in France often, by tradition, a woman. As one of them, Martine Barraqué wrote, 'The film used to change a great deal at the editing stage. He rewrote a lot of the dialogue and voice-overs.'[24] Truffaut argued that the director is the focal point of organisation and control and, through participation in all stages of the film-making process, imposes on the final product his or her 'world view.' 'A good (or *Cahiers*-approved) director was the author of a corpus of work in which every film displayed a recognisable style expressing a consistent personal vision.'[25] The concept of the *auteur* was at the heart of the New Wave but held sway only briefly before being engulfed by the emerging theoretical movements. Despite being unfashionable, an 'author' approach to film criticism is, however, still adopted by numerous critics and scholars.

The New Wave was never more than a loose association of directors who happened to come together at a critical point in time. They shared a common passion for cinema and spent long hours in discussion at the *Cinémathèque*, the various ciné clubs and the offices of the *Cahiers du cinéma*. They never formally constituted a movement nor unreservedly subscribed to an organised, coherent theory. They did, however, share a number of values and, for a while at least, an approach to film-making. Influenced by the Italian neorealists whose films they saw in their cinema clubs, they opted for a new style of realism. They turned their backs

Ecole communale du 5 rue Milton, Paris (1944)
Truffaut is sitting in the first row of chairs, third from the left. His friend Claude Thibaudat (who later performed as Claude Véga) is sitting on the far right on the same row. With Robert Lachenay, the three of them shared a love of cinema. It was not uncommon for them to 'acquire' desired stills from cinemas (see pages 43 & 134).

ABOVE
At the fairground, Paris
Truffaut (with gun) attempts to hit a bullseye while his friend Robert Lachenay (right) looks on. Two years older than Truffaut, Lachenay was a constant friend and companion through the many difficult years that Truffaut was alienated from his parents.

TOP LEFT
Filming 'Les Visiteurs du samedi soir' (1944)
When Roland Truffaut decided to make a parody of Marcel Carné's recently released 'Les Visiteurs du soir' during a mountaineering trip to Fontainebleau, François agreed to go. Here François plays the midget.

LEFT
Mountaineering at Le Puiselet in Fontainebleau forest (1944)
François Truffaut is on the far right, beside his stepfather Roland and his mother Janine. Roland and Janine met through the Club Alpin and they pursued their joint passion for mountaineering as often as they could.

on the studios and went out to shoot in the street, with natural lighting and, when it became possible, with direct sound. They avoided stars and shot their films on modest budgets. They were aided in this approach by recent technological advances and in particular by the new lightweight, portable cameras. *Les Quatre Cents Coups* provides the classic example of the new style of film: shot on the streets of Paris, in a cramped apartment, with glimpses of school life, it provided a breath of fresh air on its release in 1959. Other films in the same vein, by Chabrol, Godard, Rohmer and Rivette, appeared at about the same time and created the somewhat false impression of a concerted movement.

There were other important aspects to the New Wave, in particular its highly ambiguous relationship with American cinema. On the one hand, American directors were among those most revered by the group and the Hollywood genre approach, e.g. the gangster film, was adopted by Truffaut in *Tirez sur le pianiste* and by Godard in *A bout de souffle* (1959). On the other, they sought to create a cinema that was French, that reflected French values and showed France as it currently was.

For some time Truffaut continued to nourish ambitions of becoming a writer. Film-making, however, not only allowed him to write but also gave him the chance to draw on his immense knowledge of films and his growing awareness of how they were made. Increasingly, the desire grew to cross the line from critic to director. His first effort, in 1954, was an 8-minute short film, *Une visite*, shot with 16mm film stock obtained by Robert Lachenay, who recalls, 'I was working in a factory and with my holiday pay I bought the film stock and we shot the film. Rivette was cameraman and I was everything else: scene shifter, electrician, assistant director etc.'[27] The set was Jacques Doniol-Valcroze's flat in the rue de Douai, the actors – of whom there were four – friends. Significantly, these included a two-year-old child, Florence, the daughter of Jacques Doniol-Valcroze.

The story (described by De Baecque and Toubiana[28]) is simple: a young man moves in to share a flat with a young woman. Her brother-in-law stops by to drop off his daughter whom the woman is to babysit. He flirts with her. Later, the young man makes a clumsy pass at his co-tenant, but is rebuffed. He packs and leaves. Truffaut used the film as a training ground and did not think it worthy of distribution. The letting of a flat, a young man's clumsy flirtation with a girl and the presence of a child are all components of films to come. Above all, to amuse the young woman, the brother-in-law imitates a train by puffing cigarette smoke. A trick repeated, by a woman, seven years later in *Jules et Jim*.

The origins of Truffaut's first major film, *Les Mistons*, can be traced to September 1956 and the Venice film festival. It was there that he met Pierre Braunberger and Madeleine Morgenstern. The former was a producer with a record of backing young directors, the latter the daughter of Ignace Morgenstern, managing director of Cocinor, one of France's largest film distribution companies.

As Godard said in his film *Tout va bien* (*All's Well*, 1972), to make a film you need two things: money and a story. Truffaut had few problems finding the latter but until this point had not found a source of the former. A meeting with Maurice Pons, author of a book of short stories, was to provide the story while the developing friendship with Madeleine Morgenstern led to the funding. Truffaut liked Pons' concise, highly literary style and was attracted to the story entitled *Les Mistons*. Madeleine asked her father to help in funding the project. He passed the job to his colleague Marcel Berbert, but more importantly insisted that a company be created to receive the money and manage production of the film. Thus it was

Boulevard Saint-Michel, Paris (1948)
The Cercle Cinémane (the Film Buffs' Club) was a film club established by Robert Lachenay (left, general secretary and manager) and François Truffaut (right, artistic director) in October 1948. Truffaut got into terrible debt and left home. On 7 December his stepfather Roland caught him at a screening of John Ford's 'The Long Voyage Home' and on 10 December Truffaut was placed in the Paris Observation Centre for Minors in Villejuif. On 21 March 1949, he wrote in an essay: 'I don't gaze at the sky for long, for when I look back down again the world seems horrid to me.'

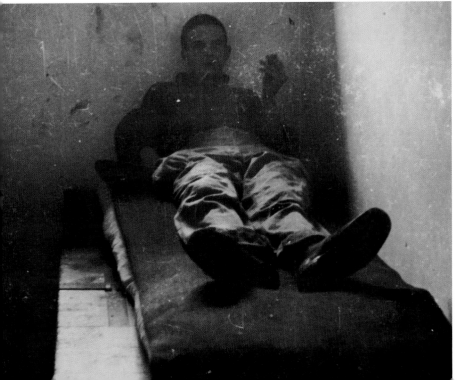

ABOVE
François Truffaut in military prison (1951)
Having enlisted and then realised that it was a mistake, Truffaut went missing several times but was picked up by the military and jailed. After a suicide attempt he was comforted by the letters and books sent by friends.

LEFT
François Truffaut in military prison (1951)
Truffaut began a correspondence with Jean Genet, who arranged for his publisher Gallimard to send Truffaut copies of their 'Série noire' thrillers. Truffaut liked the books and later adapted five novels in the series (by David Goodis, Cornell Woolrich/William Irish, Henry Farrell, Charles Williams) into films.

Still from 'Les Mistons' (1957)
The brats of the title decide to spy on Bernadette Jouve and torment her because they are too young to love her.

that the Films du Carrosse came into being. It also saw the start of Truffaut's lifelong relationship with Marcel Berbert, who was to become manager of the company. The significance of creating a company cannot be underestimated. Although the fortunes of the company waxed and waned in step with the success or otherwise of the films, it guaranteed Truffaut a crucial and almost unique independence throughout his directorial career.

Filming began in Nîmes on 2 August 1957 and continued throughout August with a small team and a modest budget. The actors were Gérard Blain – who already had a burgeoning reputation – and Bernadette Lafont, whose first cinema role it was, and five young boys selected from many. Two of Truffaut's close friends, Robert Lachenay and Claude de Givray, helped give François confidence. Much of the equipment and know-how was provided by Jean Malige, who did the photography. Originally 40 minutes long, the film was reduced in editing to 23 minutes.

The storyline is simple: a group of boys pursue and torment a young couple, Gérard and Bernadette, over the course of a hot summer in Provence. Their mischief assumes a variety of forms – spying, jeering, chasing, writing graffiti – and occurs in a number of locations – in the famous arena, at the river, at the tennis

court, in the local cinema, in the woods. At the end of the summer, the boys learn that Gérard has been killed in a mountain accident.

The delightful *Les Mistons* is a seminal work. Most of the themes that Truffaut reworked in later films are present: in particular love, children, writing and death. As in most of his work, the question of narrative structure and the telling of a story in the medium of film amounts to a theme in itself. The genre of the film is in itself an important statement. What it is not – war film, gangster film, thriller – is as significant as what it is: a slice of provincial life and a witty observation on growing up at the pre-adolescent (the kids) and the early adult (the lovers) stages. Truffaut was more at home with the almost documentary-style charting of the kids' adventures and the film constituted a first attempt at realism. As such it positioned itself as unequivocally French. This is played out in the film in terms of the juxtapositioning of a reference to the *L'Arroseur arrosé* ('The Sprinkler Sprinkled,' 1895), a silent film made by Louis Lumière, with a sequence showing the lads playing, in the arena, at gangsters/soldiers/cowboys and Indians. This 'play' is a clear allusion to Hollywood genre movies whilst the former reference is a metaphor for French cinema. *Les Mistons* is thus stating unambiguously that French cinema must be French and reflect French life, culture and people.

ABOVE
Still from 'Les Mistons' (1957)
Every Thursday, Bernadette (Bernadette Lafont) plays tennis with boyfriend Gérard. The brats are always watching her from behind the fence.

PAGE 34
On the set of 'Les Mistons' (1957)
Robert Lachenay said that Bernadette Lafont was happy to pose for him and that he was happy to take pictures.

PAGE 35
On the set of 'Les Mistons' (1957)
Bernadette Lafont and Gérard Blain, husband and wife in life, play young lovers. They meet at the Nîmes arena, where filming began on 2 August 1957.

On the set of 'Les Mistons' (1957)
On 8 August 1957, Truffaut (behind camera) filmed the scene where the lovers part at Montpellier railway station. The equipment was loaned by cameraman Jean Malige and did not have to run silently because the sound was dubbed afterwards.

The importance of writing to Truffaut has already been mentioned. It is to feature frequently as a theme throughout his work. It plays a minor but key role in *Les Mistons*: having failed to make much of an impact through hassling and harrying, the boys turn to writing graffiti and sending a postcard in the belief that the written word will carry more weight. The children themselves, their exuberance, impetuousness, lack of sexual awareness, inventive mischievousness, humour and language are at the heart of the film. Although we see Gérard and Bernadette almost exclusively through their eyes, the balance of power within the couple, their vibrant sexuality, their vulnerability are also evocatively portrayed.

The film's mature use of film language is its most lasting achievement. Like the greats before him whose films he knew by heart, Truffaut skilfully deployed music, dialogue, lighting, setting, objects and actors to create a cogent, powerful narrative. The structure is deliberately episodic, less a movement from a beginning to an end than a repeated circling around and progressive deepening of his themes. Repetition and variation sustain the film. We first see Bernadette on her bike in the streets of Nîmes passing though light and shadow. Shortly afterwards, as Gérard is presented, the light and shadows are again there, but he is walking. The female is graceful, fluent, in smooth movement, the male on foot, slower, having less *élan*.

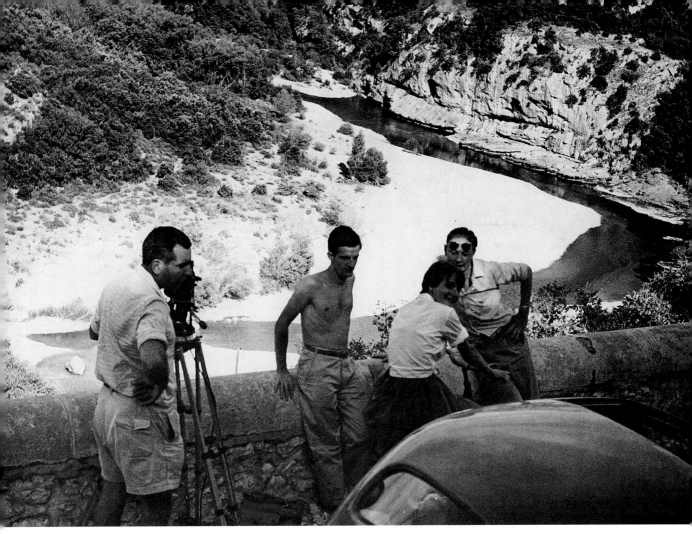

ABOVE
On the set of 'Les Mistons' (1957)
Cameraman Jean Malige, François Truffaut and assistant director Claude de Givray watch Bernadette Lafont prepare to let her skirt fly as she rides her bicycle at speed.

LEFT
On the set of 'Les Mistons' (1957)
Towards the end of the shoot, Truffaut gained confidence and was nicknamed 'the little corporal' because he resembled Napoléon at the bridge of Arcole. He had made the journey from film critic to film director.

The film was edited in early autumn of 1957 and first shown on 17 November. In between, in October, Truffaut married Madeleine. *Les Mistons* met with immediate success and won him Best Director at the Brussels World Film Festival. His next venture, *Une histoire d'eau*, was another short, made in the spring of 1958. The idea for this 10-minute film was prompted by floods in the Paris region of which Truffaut took some footage. The project was then taken over by Godard, who edited it, intervening at the levels of narrative structure and dialogue. Although Godard's contribution was much the greater, the film was co-signed.

The success of *Les Mistons* brought Truffaut recognition and more importantly, further financial backing. Although he had not particularly liked the film, Ignace Morgenstern put up the money for another film. Truffaut turned to another of his scenarios on childhood and began work on the script of *Les Quatre Cents Coups*, eventually enlisting the help of Marcel Moussy, an experienced writer. They quickly completed the scenario and Truffaut set about casting. Shooting began in November 1958, sadly coinciding with the death of Truffaut's mentor, André Bazin, and was completed on 5 January 1959. Chosen as one of three films to represent France at the Cannes Film Festival, it was shown there on 4 May and released in Paris on 3 June.

The narrative structure is again episodic rather than linear. Antoine, a young boy living in Paris in the 1950s, inhabits a small flat with his mother, Gilberte, and stepfather, Julien. From a series of scenes in the flat, at school, in the streets and at a detention centre, we gradually piece together a picture of Antoine's childhood. His mother, resentful of a child she had not wanted, is alternately loving and cruel. She is insensitive to his needs and uncaring of a child passing through the difficult time of puberty. She has lovers. The stepfather is capable of sharing jokes with Antoine and spending time with him. However, he lacks patience, striking him forcibly at one point and later turning him over to the police. There is no relief at school, where Antoine's truancy and independent nature bring him into conflict with the teachers. He turns for consolation to his friend René Bigey and we see them involved in a series of escapades: smoking in René's bedroom, stealing money from René's mother, visiting a fair and stealing a typewriter. This last act prompts the stepfather to hand Antoine over to the police. There follows a night in police cells and a stay in a remand home near the coast. Antoine takes the opportunity during a games lesson to flee the home and run to the sea. In the last shot of the film, having reached the water he turns back towards the land – and the camera – and is caught in a final freeze-frame.

It is easy to identify the intimate and autobiographical nature of the material. The film is in many ways the epitome of the neorealism promoted by the New Wave, capturing the 'extraordinary quality of ordinary situations.' The settings were immediately familiar to the audience: school, flat, street, behaviour of pupils and teachers, relationships with parents and authority, the rebellious nature of an unruly and marginalised child. The film is dominated by the young boy's relationship with his mother and stepfather and particularly the former. He is seduced by her beauty and disturbed by her sexuality, which she flaunts in front of him. His love is not returned and she spurns him time and again. His vision of her as beautiful and pure nevertheless survives until the day he sees her embracing a lover in the street. Julien, who in earshot of Antoine chides his wife for her extramarital adventures, devotes most of his time and energy to rally driving. His easygoing behaviour contrasts sharply and, for Antoine, confusingly, with sudden brutal outbursts.

**Jean-Luc Godard, Suzanne Schiffman &
François Truffaut**
Truffaut met Godard and Schiffman in Paris in 1949, along with other lovers of film. Many of them began publishing articles in 'Cahiers du cinéma', a film magazine edited by André Bazin, one of Truffaut's mentors.

ABOVE
Still from 'Une histoire d'eau' (1958)
This humorous short film about a man (Jean-Claude Brialy) and woman (Caroline Dim) trying to drive through blocked roads and flooded fields was shot in two days on the outskirts of Montereau.

LEFT
Still from 'Une histoire d'eau' (1958)
The film was directed by Truffaut at the last minute to take advantage of the flood, and to fill his time before starting a film that was never made. Jean-Luc Godard edited the film and supplied the voice of the man.

ABOVE
Still from 'Les Quatre Cents Coups' (1959)
René Bigey (Patrick Auffay) and Antoine Doinel
(Jean-Pierre Léaud) see Antoine's mother (Claire
Maurier) kissing a man from her office (Jean
Douchet). Antoine's relationship with his mother,
specifically the lack of love that he receives from
her, is the subtext for a lot of the film.

RIGHT
Still from 'Les Quatre Cents Coups' (1959)
Antoine sits at his mother's dressing table and
sniffs some of her perfume. It is as if he is
investigating her because he does not know her.
Truffaut often uses mirrors in his films (see
pages 1, 58, 93, 96 & 163).

Still from 'Les Quatre Cents Coups' (1959)
Antoine excuses his absence from school by telling his teacher that his mother is dead. (In a sense this is true, just as he is dead to her. He is in her way and Truffaut shows this when she has to literally step over him to get into their apartment.) This is the moment when Antoine is called to the back of the classroom to be slapped by his stepfather for telling such a wicked lie.

LEFT
Still from 'Les Quatre Cents Coups' (1959)
In the centre for juvenile delinquents, Antoine waits anxiously for his friend René to visit him, but René is refused entry. Antoine is disappointed that his mother is allowed to see him. She really is dead to him now.

Still from 'Les Quatre Cents Coups' (1959)
Antoine and René steal a typewriter (just as Truffaut had stolen a typewriter from the Boy Scouts) but cannot sell it. Although the inexperienced Antoine and the knowledgeable René were partially based on the relationship between Truffaut and Lachenay, in reality Lachenay was the leader and Truffaut was shy. When Jean-Pierre Léaud was cast as Antoine, his dominant personality greatly influenced the character and Truffaut made changes to reflect that.

Still from 'Les Quatre Cents Coups' (1959)
Antoine and René steal a still of Monika (Harriet Andersson) in Ingmar Bergman's 'Summer with Monika' (1953). At the end of 'Les Quatre Cents Coups' Antoine looks directly into the camera, just as Monika had looked into the camera.

"I am much less autobiographical than people think."

François Truffaut [29]

Left often to his own devices, Antoine transgresses. School is presented more as a prison than a place of learning. The teachers are either weak or harshly authoritarian. Police and remand home offer no respite. Of the adults, only the female psychologist shows genuine sympathy and understanding. Otherwise, Antoine's only solace comes from his friendship with René – the study of male friendship is an important component of this and other Truffaut films. Despite the bleak world Antoine inhabits, there are moments of elation, mostly associated with culture: the visit to the Gaumont-Palace (to see a Rivette film), the Punch and Judy show with its shots of pure joy on infant faces, and Antoine's delight in reading Balzac.

This brings us again to writing as theme. It is present in many forms: school essays, reading novels and forging letters to explain truancy. For the most part, these constitute an attempt to see or present the world differently, to reshape the reality experienced. Writing is creative, a source of happiness.

Despite these lighter moments and the rich vein of humour that runs through it, *Les Quatre Cents Coups* is for the most part a bleak film. The ending, however, is ambiguous: Antoine reaches the sea, which he had never previously seen, but immediately turns back to the land. Freedom is achieved but is dull, desolate, disorienting. However, Antoine has come through his various ordeals and the expression on his face can be read as one of defiance and determination to survive.

The film was an enormous success, handsomely repaying his father-in-law's investment. Truffaut and his team took Cannes by storm, with Truffaut winning the award for Best Director. More significantly, it helped provoke a general shift in French society to a youth-oriented culture and brought to the attention of critics and audiences alike the methods and principles of the New Wave. And not only French audiences, for very quickly the film attracted distributors worldwide and was showing in New York, London, Tokyo and Rome. Almost overnight, Truffaut and the New Wave had moved onto the world stage. He was just 27.

There were other consequences. Unsurprisingly, Janine and Roland Truffaut demanded that their 'son' visit to explain himself. Truffaut's income shot up dramatically, bringing lifestyle changes: clothes, sports car, a new and larger flat in the 16th *arrondissement*, travel. He began collecting records and, particularly, books. His new-found wealth enabled him to support Rivette, Godard – who used a ten-page Truffaut synopsis for *A bout de souffle* – and Claude de Givray, for whom he produced two films. In October he went to London for the English première of *Les Quatre Cents Coups*, gaining a lifelong friend in Richard Roud. The following January he was in New York for the American première and to receive that city's Critics Award for Best Foreign Film. He met Helen Scott, press officer at the French Film Office, who was to become one of his greatest supporters and collaborated with him to produce the book on Hitchcock. If he was momentarily carried away with his success, he was brought down to earth when he wrote off his sports car in an accident in 1962.

"When they are finished, I realise that my films are always sadder than I intended."

François Truffaut [30]

ABOVE
On the set of 'Les Quatre Cents Coups' (1959)
Truffaut left all the scenes with the children to
the end of the shoot, when he was more
confident. Here he is playing with Richard
Kanayan, who would be in Truffaut's next film.

OPPOSITE
On the set of 'Les Quatre Cents Coups' (1959)
François Truffaut and Jean-Pierre Léaud would
make a 20-year cycle of Antoine Doinel films.

"Where did I find the name Antoine Doinel? For a long time I really did believe that I had invented it until the day someone pointed out to me that I had simply borrowed it from Jean Renoir's secretary, Ginette Doynel!"

François Truffaut [31]

ABOVE
On the set of 'Les Quatre Cents Coups' (1959)
Cameraman Henri Decaë is strapped to the central post of the rotator for the fairground scene.

RIGHT
On the set of 'Les Quatre Cents Coups' (1959)
Léaud, Lachenay and Truffaut discuss the scene where Antoine will climb up the wall. Truffaut has a cameo appearance inside the rotator.

On the set of 'Les Quatre Cents Coups' (1959)
The famous final scene where Antoine runs to
the sea was filmed in Normandy. The film shoot
began on 10 November 1958. That evening the
great film critic André Bazin, Truffaut's mentor
and father-figure, died. Filming ended on 5
January 1959. On 22 January, Truffaut's first
child, Laura, was born. On the evening of 4 May
'Les Quatre Cents Coups' was the toast of
Cannes.

A Hymn to Life and Death
1960–1963

Finance for his next project was more readily forthcoming, though *Tirez sur le pianiste* was to cost twice as much as *Les Quatre Cents Coups*. In part, this was due to the cost of buying the rights of *Down There*, a crime novel by American David Goodis, and of hiring Charles Aznavour for the role of Charlie Koller. Truffaut again worked with Marcel Moussy on the scenario, completing it in July 1959. His team was quickly assembled. Raoul Coutard did the photography. Suzanne Schiffman, whom Truffaut had met at the *Cinémathèque*, did continuity, thus beginning a working relationship that lasted until Truffaut's death. Albert Rémy, the father from *Les Quatre Cents Coups*, played the role of Chico; Michèle Mercier, the prostitute Clarisse. In the auditions, Truffaut was struck by a young actress called Claudine Huzé. Adopting the stage name Marie Dubois, she was taken on to play Léna (and Thérèse in Truffaut's next film).

Chico Saroyan and his brother Richard have committed a crime with accomplices, Momo and Ernest. The Saroyans have double-crossed their partners who are hot in pursuit of Chico. He takes refuge in a bar where another of his brothers is resident pianist. At first, his brother ignores him, but gives in and helps him escape. Our attention switches to the brother, living under the assumed name of Charlie Koller. Charlie lives with a fourth younger brother, Fido, and occasionally shares his bed with Clarisse, a prostitute. Léna, a waitress at the bar, who is in love with Charlie, takes him back to her flat. She knows that he was formerly Edouard Saroyan, a renowned concert pianist. In a flashback, we learn that earlier in his life he had married Thérésa, also a waitress. She encouraged him to take up a career as a pianist and in order to secure him a contract with impresario Lars Schmeel, slept with the latter. Discovering this later, Edouard is unable to handle the situation and leaves her. She commits suicide. Returning to the present, Charlie gets into a fight over Léna with Plyne, owner of the bar. Plyne is killed. Meanwhile Momo and Ernest have kidnapped Fido. With the help of Léna, Charlie flees to the family's mountain home where they meet up with Chico and Richard. Momo and Ernest arrive and a gunfight ensues in the course of which Léna is killed. Charlie returns to his job as pianist in the bar now run by Mammy, Plyne's wife, who introduces him to a new waitress.

The opening sequence takes up again, from *Les Mistons*, Truffaut's ambiguous relationship with American cinema. First signs indicate that we are watching a *film*

"I firmly believe that we must refuse any hierarchisation of genres and consider that what is 'cultural' is simply everything which pleases us, entertains us, interests us, helps us to live. 'All films are born free and equal,' as André Bazin once wrote."

François Truffaut [32]

ABOVE
Still from 'Tirez sur le pianiste' (1960)
Truffaut mixed the conventions of 'film noir' with those of human drama. Here Charlie fights Plyne (Serge Davri) in a battle between knife and telephone. They are fighting because the ugly but sensitive Plyne ("I'm nobody's type") is in love with Léna (right) and is angry that she and Charlie slept together.

OPPOSITE TOP
Still from 'Tirez sur le pianiste' (1960)
The film begins with Chico Saroyan (Albert Rémy) running for his life and then bumping into a lamppost. A passerby (Alex Joffé) helps him up and tells him how he fell in love with his wife two years after he married her. The change of pace (quick to slow) and tone (thriller to romance) immediately shows Truffaut's ironic intent for the film.

OPPOSITE BOTTOM LEFT
Still from 'Tirez sur le pianiste' (1960)
Charlie is a shy womaniser. He is seduced by Léna, the waitress at the bar where he plays piano, who knows that he used to be concert pianist Edouard Saroyan. Charlie recounts the tragic events that led to his wife's suicide.

OPPOSITE BOTTOM RIGHT
Still from 'Tirez sur le pianiste' (1960)
Charlie has an informal relationship with Clarisse (Michèle Mercier), a prostitute who lives next door. She undresses behind the screen ("Ain't they cute?" she says showing her panties) and then Truffaut shows her breasts when she is in bed with Charlie. They joke that in the movies, you don't see the breasts.

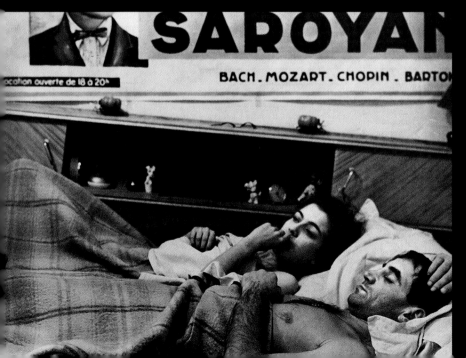

noir – car chase, night, the city with its wet streets and pools of light, rapid cutting. But our assumptions are immediately called into question by a two-minute continuous tracking shot in which Chico and a stranger discuss love and marriage. The preoccupation with genre does not however fade away, rather it becomes more complex as elements of other genres infiltrate the narrative. The iconography of the musical, comedy and western each features briefly. The effect on the spectator is disorienting. What are we watching? What is the director playing at? For playing he clearly is. There are numerous allusions to films past and present, like the triple-screen reference to Abel Gance, and at one point Charlie speaks directly to the audience. Moreover, disruption of genre occurs also on the level of tone: the film is frequently very funny, with moments of farce. But alongside these are darker moments, closer to tragedy, as when Thérésa takes her own life and Léna is shot.

Truffaut, we come quickly to understand, is not so much making a genre film as he is subverting one. The profusion of apparently random, heterogeneous components form only the outer layer of the film. At its heart lie themes central to Truffaut's worldview: the elation and despair of love; the complexity of the 'couple' relationship; the shy, hesitant male (Charlie); the strong decisive female (Thérésa and Léna); and chauvinist attitudes to women. The interest in children and childhood is also present, mainly through Fido and his pragmatic, wry take on the world he inhabits. Although in many respects this is one of the least realist of Truffaut's films, there is nonetheless an emblematic presence of contemporary Paris: the bar, the dance, the flat, the cars.

Truffaut's aim of subverting genre is evident in the manner in which he set about transposing David Goodis' novel. His approach typifies his attitude to adaptation: he was drawn to the novel because it portrayed characters, attitudes and locations of a type he appreciated. However, having read the book, he discarded it and took only what interested him, transforming the original in the process. The film becomes his and the novel only an inspiration, never a straitjacket, as it might have been for directors of the 'tradition of quality.' Perhaps the film's main theme is once again film itself. The director seems to be asking us 'what is cinema?' and in a style typical of Truffaut, involving us directly in the formulation of an answer.

ABOVE
On the set of 'Tirez sur le pianiste' (1960)
Charles Aznavour, François Truffaut, Serge Davri (with knife sticking out of his back) and Marie Dubois (in background).

OPPOSITE
Still from 'Tirez sur le pianiste' (1960)
Charlie beats Plyne and then throws away the knife, but Plyne's machismo will not allow it. Plyne says that he can't back down now and starts strangling Charlie, saying, "Women are wonderful. Women are supreme," but that Léna is now a slut. He is expressing some of the sentiments that Charlie had, and which led to the suicide of Charlie's wife.

RIGHT
On the set of 'Jules et Jim' (1962)
François Truffaut lines up a shot of the statue
that intrigues Jules and Jim. They are attracted
to her smile and they vow that if they see that
smile on a woman they will follow it.

ABOVE
Still from 'Jules et Jim' (1962)
When Jules and Jim (Henri Serre, right) meet
Catherine (Jeanne Moreau) they immediately
recognise the smile that they must follow. Jules
marries her, but then she wants to sleep with
Jim.

Tirez sur le pianiste was not well received. Few saw the coherence underlying the surface complexity or appreciated the skilful binding together of the personal and the aesthetic. With one success and one failure from his two feature-length films, it was back to the drawing board. At most stages in his career, Truffaut had more than one scenario under treatment. He turned now to a project he had been preparing for some time: another adaptation, this time of Henri-Pierre Roché's novel *Jules et Jim*. Truffaut was drawn to Roché for reasons similar to those that had attracted him to Maurice Pons: elegance of style and shared themes. Following Truffaut's excursions into production, the financial support he gave colleagues and the failure of a costly film, the Films du Carrosse was passing through a shaky period, the more so since Ignace Morgenstern had died. Berbert procured funds for distribution rights, enabling work to begin. The budget was very modest and locations were often provided by friends. With the exception of Jeanne Moreau, the actors were, in keeping with New Wave practice, virtual unknowns.

Truffaut was not satisfied with his scenario and eventually turned to Jean Gruault, whose work he knew and liked. This was the first of many occasions on which Gruault would work with Truffaut. The team was quickly assembled. Berbert took the crucial role of producer. Many of the crew from *Tirez sur le pianiste* were retained, creating the 'family' atmosphere that Truffaut was already beginning to favour. Suzanne Schiffman stayed on as 'continuity girl,' as did Claudine Bouché as editor. Coutard was again responsible for photography. Georges Delerue contributed another highly distinctive score. Henri Serre, tall and elegant, landed the role of Jim and the German actor Oskar Werner that of Jules. Marie Dubois reappeared (as Thérèse) and a girl by the name of Sabine Haudepin played Jules and Catherine's daughter. Friends such as Jean-Louis Richard took minor roles. The film was shot in Paris and in the south of France, mostly within reach of Jeanne Moreau's house at La Garde-Freinet.

In the Paris of the *belle époque*, friends Jules and Jim share everything, including women. Seeing a friend's slides of classical statues, they are both struck by one of a smiling woman. They visit the original and, on returning to Paris, meet Catherine, who has the smile of the statue. Jules courts her and warns Jim that this one is not for sharing. Jules tells Jim of his intention to marry Catherine and move to his native Germany. The war intervenes. When it ends, Jim visits them at their chalet; they now have a daughter, Sabine. Catherine, restless, seduces Jim. Jules accepts the situation. Jim returns to Paris promising to return to be with Catherine but letters cross, intentions are misunderstood. He returns to Germany; Catherine tries in vain to conceive his child. Their relationship sours. Catherine turns to Albert, a guitar-playing friend. Jim leaves. Years later, Jim meets Jules and Catherine by chance in a cinema. Shortly afterwards, she entices Jim into her car and drives off a ruined bridge, killing them both. At their funeral Jules, alone, holds their ashes.

Jules et Jim is, on the surface, another genre film in that it is a period drama, set in the first 30 years or so of the twentieth century. As with *Les Mistons*, this is again an adaptation but, as with Pons' short story, Truffaut takes only what he wants from Roché's novel. In a manner now becoming familiar, both genre and novel serve as vehicles for the expression of his ideas. He made this clear himself: 'Unless the characters are interesting, the film won't be either. The historical setting is of only minor importance.'[34] The film is in a sense an epic, spanning three decades, two countries and the Great War. It deals with major themes like love,

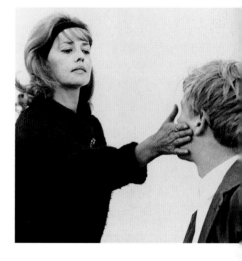

ABOVE
Still from 'Jules et Jim' (1962)
When Jules and Jim do not pay attention to Catherine, she slaps Jules (Oskar Werner) and then begins laughing. She tells them: "Before I met you I never laughed."

OPPOSITE
Still from 'Jules et Jim' (1962)
Catherine disguises herself as 'Thomas' because only men are free to do as they want.

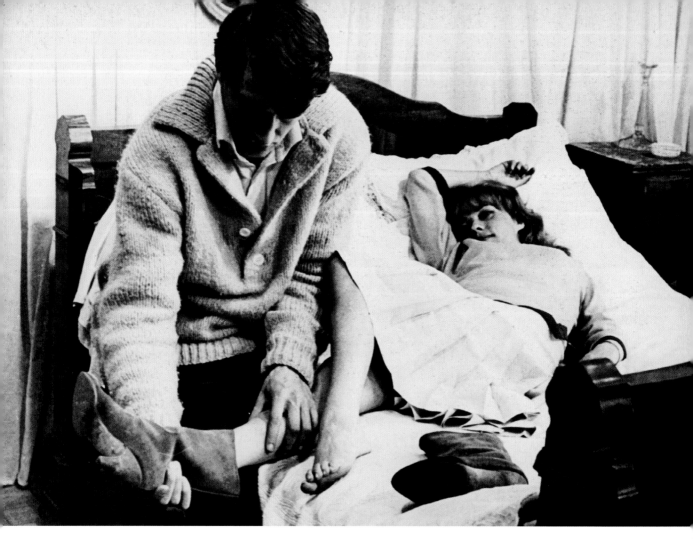

ABOVE
Still from 'Jules et Jim' (1962)
Although Catherine seems docile at times, it is she who selects and seduces Jim. She has arranged her world so that she is free to do as she pleases.

RIGHT
Still from 'Jules et Jim' (1962)
Catherine knits as her three men, Albert (Boris Bassiak, aka singer Serge Rezvani), Jim and Jules, wait to do her bidding.

ABOVE
Still from 'Jules et Jim' (1962)
After watching a Swedish play, the men are not impressed. However, Catherine says: "I like that girl! She wants to be free and live each moment of her life."

LEFT
Still from 'Jules et Jim' (1962)
Jules and Jim talk about the men in the Swedish play and Jules repeats anti-female quotes. The men are ignoring the female character, and degrading her. In protest, Catherine throws herself in the water, prefiguring her suicide.

On the set of 'Jules et Jim' (1962)
François Truffaut looks through the window, like many of his characters (see page 23).

friendship, happiness and death. As its creator declared in a letter to Helen Scott, it is 'a hymn to life and death.'[35]

Three comments from the director are helpful in capturing his inspiration for this film. In the first, Truffaut writes, 'There is a song in the film: it is called *Le Tourbillon de la vie* (*The Whirlwind of Life*); it sets the tone for the film and is the key to it.'[36] In a scene in the chalet in Germany, Catherine sings the song accompanied by Albert, another of her lovers, on his guitar. The role was taken by Serge Rezvani, who also wrote the song. The words movingly underscore the film's moods and themes: 'We got to know each other once, and then a second time, we lost contact once and then again, we met up again, and brought each other warmth, then we separated, each, alone, setting off again in the whirlwind of life…' The tune punctuates the film and brings it to a close. In a second comment, Truffaut explains how, like Roché in his novel, he was exploring alternatives to the couple: 'It is also a film about love based on the theory that, since the couple is not always a successful and satisfactory proposition, it seems legitimate to look for a different morality, other ways of living, even if any other arrangement is destined to fail.'[37] Finally he notes, '[Love] is the most important subject. It is *the* subject. You could well devote half of your career to it (as Bergman did) or three-quarters of it (like Renoir). Because every love story has something to say, just as every love is unique.'[38]

As Truffaut acknowledged, the film stands or falls on its characters. And these do not disappoint. Catherine in particular is a major achievement. A strong, intelligent, highly strung, highly sexual woman, she is one of Jeanne Moreau's most successful roles. It certainly confirmed her emerging reputation as one of France's most gifted actresses. It is not by accident that the name of Catherine does not feature in the film's title. In part this is due to the fact that we are not given direct access to her thoughts and mind. We see her almost exclusively through the eyes of Jules and Jim. This may, in large part, explain her apparently aberrant, wilful behaviour. The chauvinist attitudes of these decades forced women into a narrow social space from which Catherine repeatedly erupts: dressing as a man, cheating, setting fire to herself, jumping in the Seine, swapping partners, pointing guns and, finally, killing both herself and Jim. Only when we identify and accept the political, social and physical repression of women can we come to understand the character and, arguably, the film.

The male characters are equally well drawn, although neither is the equal of Catherine. Jules, gentle, tolerant to a fault, idolises his wife and accepts her taking lovers if it means she does not leave him. Jim is of a different breed. More charismatic and dynamic than his friend, he too, however, eventually proves indecisive. The very male nature of their friendship is evoked in small details: their sharing of tastes, their broad passion for various forms of culture, for sport and for women.

The theme of writing recurs and plays a major part in the film: Jules at the outset is writing a novel based on his friendship with Jim. He later becomes a botanist and writer. Jim is a journalist of stature. Letters are central to theme and plot development, charting the missed opportunities, reflecting, even causing, the misunderstandings. The success of the film can also be attributed to Truffaut's growing command of film language. *Jules et Jim* has a coherence, a seamless quality which stems from the almost invisible way in which the cinematic devices combine to underscore the themes. Space precludes an extended analysis here.[39] However, cursory and selective reference to the importance of the music, to camera movement and angle, frame composition, objects used as metaphors (like bicycles, windows, the statue, water, vitriol) and shapes such as the circle/broken circles, hint at the contribution of the film's formal elements to its meaning.

Released on 24 January 1962, *Jules et Jim* was hampered by its '18' certificate and had only moderate success. It was then, briefly, banned in Italy. However, the now obligatory promotional tour and hard work by agents eventually assured the film the success and box-office receipts it merited.

"I make ordinary films for ordinary people."

François Truffaut [40]

On the set of 'Jules et Jim' (1962)
Jeanne Moreau gave François Truffaut courage each time he had doubts and helped to create the right atmosphere for their collaboration.

Still from 'Jules et Jim' (1962)
Catherine challenges Jim and Jules to a race
and then wins because, characteristically, she
does not play by the rules.

On the set of 'Jules et Jim' (1962)
Filming Jeanne Moreau, Oskar Werner and
Henri Serre with a mobile camera. The sense of
movement and pace in the film is achieved
through camera movement and rapid editing.
The camera always moves freely around
Catherine, giving her a lightness and 'joie de
vivre.' She lives each moment of her life.

While he was working on the scenario of *Jules et Jim*, often at Jeanne Moreau's house, the two had a passionate if brief affair. Upon completion of the film it had become a friendship that was to prove close and enduring. Typically, Truffaut had already begun work on his next project. Commissioned by producer Pierre Roustang, Truffaut was to make a short film to be presented with four others in a compilation entitled *L'Amour à vingt ans*. Exhausted after *Jules et Jim* and declaring he lacked inspiration, he nevertheless set about putting his sketch together. He returned to the story of Antoine Doinel and to a scenario of his own creation. Schiffman, Coutard, Bouché and Delerue again form the 'team.' Jean-Pierre Léaud and Patrick Auffay retained the roles of Antoine and René; a 17-year-old newcomer, Marie-France Pisier, got the title role of Colette. Shot very quickly in January 1962 in Paris, *L'Amour à vingt ans* was released the following July. Truffaut, with Claudine Bouché, edited all five contributions. To Truffaut's disappointment, it did not have much success and was quickly withdrawn.

Despite its poor reception, *Antoine et Colette* is a charming, intelligent, beautifully made film suffused with Delerue's lyrical score and the haunting melody of Yvon Samuel's title song. Antoine is now 17, living alone in a flat and working in a record factory. He and René swap stories of their amorous pursuits. Antoine is infatuated with Colette, a girl he has met at youth concerts. She gives him little encouragement but, blind in his attachment, he fails to take her hints. The film ends with him staying to watch a concert on TV with her parents while she goes out with her boyfriend.

The film has much the same appeal as *Les Quatre Cents Coups*: again there is a sharp, contemporary realism and a Paris readily recognisable to its French audience. The director's deep affection for the city in which he lives is almost tangible: its boulevards, cafés, buses, cinemas, buildings and flats are evoked in a way that lends the film, particularly in retrospect, an almost documentary feel. The youth culture of the 1960s is brought vividly to life: the music (classical and pop), the gramophone, the 'surprise-parties,' telephone calls, talks in cafés, visits to the cinema, a first taste of independence and, inevitably, of love. The authenticity is guaranteed by the role Truffaut's own experiences play in the film, though as has already been pointed out, a number of them have been modified. Our sympathy for Antoine is maintained although the ironic detachment of author from protagonist has widened. We recognise, laugh at and excuse Antoine's almost grotesque fumblings, his clumsiness and misreadings of situations. The outcome of his courtship is clear long before its poignant ending as the tall, manly Albert plucks away Colette while Antoine seeks solace in television and parents.

That Truffaut is beginning to set up a series of linked films, reminiscent on a minor scale of Balzac's *Human Comedy* and Emile Zola's *Rougon-Macquart* novels, is reinforced on several levels. One of the most effective being the use of a flashback to *Les Quatre Cents Coups*. Truffaut displays a confident mastery of narrative structure and his film has all the qualities of an excellent short story: concise, spare, with its themes underpinned by a rich vein of imagery and uncommented but evocative patterns of repetition and variation. The film is only 29 minutes long but is a considerable achievement, indicative of Truffaut's stature in 1962 as a mature film-maker with an international reputation.

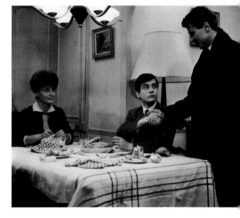

You Love Celluloid Itself
1964–1969

January 1962 brought a sharp downturn in the fortunes of the New Wave. Each director now had an individual reputation and his own ideas. The movement only ever had the most tenuous cohesion, so it is hardly surprising that a spectacular and widely reported libel case involving Truffaut, Roger Vadim and Brigitte Bardot provided a vehicle for the press to declare the New Wave dead. The young were no longer young; the critics had become directors, each with their own future.

Shortly after the trial, Truffaut visited New York with Madeleine. He was beginning to take seriously the idea of a book on Hitchcock. He approached Helen Scott to act as interpreter and wrote to Hitchcock in June 1962, 'Many directors love cinema, but you love celluloid itself and that's what I would like to talk to you about.'[41] Hitchcock agreed to a taped conversation answering a set of prepared questions. It took three years, but the book was published in New York and Paris in 1966–67 and was highly successful.

Truffaut had long been drawn to American directors and to Hitchcock above all. Four of his next five films reflect this influence, both thematically and formally. Both Hitchcock and Truffaut use genre to convey personal concerns, avoiding political or social themes to focus on love and relationships. Both concentrate on character rather than plot and stimulate interest through suspense. The legacy of silent films is important to both and there is consequently an emphasis on visual rather than verbal narration. Wry humour is common to both, and Truffaut followed Hitchcock in using Bernard Herrmann for his scores.

In less than a month, in the summer of 1963, Jean-Louis Richard put together the scenario for *La Peau douce*. The usual suspects feature in the credits, along with Léaud as a trainee-assistant. On the surface the film owes much to newspaper stories recounting a dramatic murder in a Paris restaurant. On another level, it has roots in Truffaut's conflicts over what he experienced as the hypocrisy of married life. His impetus for making the movie was to imagine the point of view of the jilted wife as opposed to that of the young mistress which was a more frequent perspective in movies on the subject.

Pierre Lachenay, renowned academic and TV personality, lives in Paris with his wife Franca and daughter Sabine. On a trip to Lisbon to give a lecture he meets Nicole, an air hostess. Back in Paris, they begin an affair. Nicole accompanies him to Reims where he is to introduce a film on Gide. Pierre takes photos of Nicole and

On the set of 'La Peau douce' (1964)
Truffaut seems to be asking for silence so that actor Jean Desailly can continue his nap. In fact, Desailly needed all the sleep he could get because after filming during the day he would act in the theatre at night. To keep costs as low as possible, Truffaut filmed the family scenes in his own apartment.

"I have often been accused of portraying weak men and decisive women, women who direct events, but I think that's how it is in real life."
François Truffaut [42]

73

Still from 'La Peau douce' (1964)
Flight stewardess Nicole (Françoise Dorléac) meets married intellectual Pierre Lachenay (Jean Desailly) and they begin an affair. Pierre then agrees to do various appearances so that he can be with Nicole while he is away.

Still from 'La Peau douce' (1964)
When Pierre travels to do his talks, he is always tied up with dinners and parties given by the organisers. Consequently, Nicole is kept waiting by Pierre, which she hates. (In the background, Jean Cocteau's 'Testament of Orpheus,' which Truffaut co-produced, is playing at the cinema.)

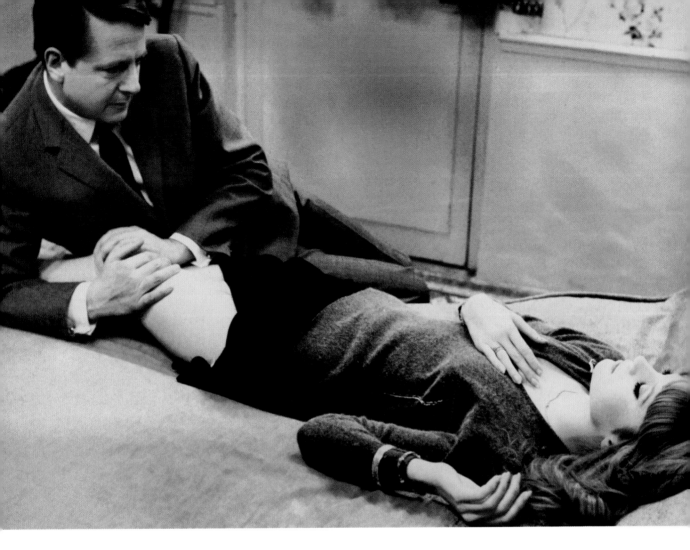

Still from 'La Peau douce' (1964)

Eventually Pierre and Nicole manage to consummate their relationship. Pierre caresses Nicole's soft skin. Truffaut liked to show women's legs. Further examples are on pages 62, 96, 124, 152/153, 168, 172 & 178,

himself. Franca discovers he was not in Reims, they argue and he leaves her. He turns to Nicole but she declares that their relationship would never work. Franca finds the receipt for the photos and picks them up. She goes to the crowded restaurant where Pierre is lunching alone. Throwing the photos at him, she shoots him with a rifle.

La Peau douce is one of Truffaut's bleakest films. A tale of adultery, shot in grainy black and white, mostly in a decidedly unromanticised Paris, its characters are unremittingly mediocre. Location, characters and story are immediately recognisable. Truffaut explains, 'The proportion of the film which is purely fictional is relatively small because I prefer to work from facts as they are presented in newspapers or from events I have experienced myself or which I have been told by acquaintances. I like my films to be authenticated by life.'[43]

Pierre is a successful academic and a public figure. In his private life, however, and particularly in the conduct of his affair, he is weak, indecisive, self-centred, terrified of being found out. Nicole's feelings for him are genuine but she is continually let down by this man who does not know his own mind. So weak is he that their lovemaking is repeatedly and frustratingly postponed, as he becomes embroiled in awkward situations of his own making. Franca is the only strong personality, "I do not like ambiguous situations," she tells her husband,

unambiguously. In the continual tension between the provisional and the absolute,
which is worked out in many of Truffaut's films, Franca is at one extreme: the
absolute. Her action in publicly killing her husband is wholly in keeping with her
refusal to accept compromise.

At a point when he was already low, Truffaut's private life now entered a period
of turmoil. The Films du Carrosse was struggling, and early in 1965 Madeleine
finally asked for a divorce. This was effected amicably but the Carrosse lost its
offices. Truffaut quickly found other premises, in the rue Robert-Estienne. He had
six projects on the go, only two of which came to fruition. He was offered *Bonnie
and Clyde* (1967) and worked on the script before turning it down.

One of his projects was *Fahrenheit 451*, the gestation period for which proved
long and difficult. The problems centred on the rights to Ray Bradbury's novel, the
costs involved in shooting a science-fiction film and casting. The film was shot in
England, mainly at Pinewood, despite Truffaut's disparaging views about English
cinema and actors. It was not a happy shoot: Truffaut's hitherto good relationship
with Oskar Werner broke down; he was frustrated by his inability to work on the
dialogue of this foreign-language film.

Truffaut claimed that the scenario owed 60% to Bradbury's novel and 40% to
himself. The adaptation was the product of another collaboration with Jean-Louis

Richard, though David Rudkin, the English playwright, and Helen Scott both contributed. The film is set in the future in an unidentified location. Montag, a fireman whose job is to find and burn books, is married to Linda. He is good at his work and is in line for promotion. They live in a totalitarian and repressive society. A young neighbour, Clarisse, talks to Montag on the monorail on the way back from work. Montag is frustrated with the passive, shallow and narcissistic Linda. He reads *David Copperfield* in secret. Clarisse unsettles him further, asking him why he does such an unpleasant job. He begins reading extensively; Linda makes him choose between her and his books. Clarisse's aunt and uncle, with whom she lives, are arrested but Clarisse escapes. She tells Montag about communities of people who preserve books by learning them by heart. She is leaving to join one of these and invites Montag to go with her. He says he is not ready. He becomes more and more distracted at work. Linda reveals to the authorities that Montag has books in the house. Montag participates in the raid on his own house. He turns his flame-thrower on the Captain and flees to join the book people, and Clarisse.

At first sight, *Fahrenheit 451* is a science-fiction film – a reading confirmed by the conventional iconography: the monorail, absence of the written word, the echoes of 'Big Brother,' firemen whose job it is to start fires rather than put them out, flying police. However, it quickly becomes apparent that the sci-fi component is a thin veneer. The fire engine looks like something from an early silent movie, and the uniforms are more reminiscent of the Nazis than the future. Even in 1966, there was nothing novel about a Big Brother mentality. Truffaut instructed Bernard Herrmann, the composer, to write 'a dramatic score in a traditional and not futuristic style.'[44] There was, he claimed, only one truly sci-fi sequence: that involving the flying police. Everything conspires to puncture the sci-fi façade e.g. moments of humour such as the lingering on a TV programme which Linda is avidly soaking up but which comprises monotonous repetition of phrases from an English-language textbook. Even the fire fighters' symbol – the fire-resistant salamander – is ironic.

So what attracted Truffaut to Bradbury's novel, and why did he turn to this genre? In large part, it was his own attraction to literature, the importance he attached to the written word, and his horror at the Nazis' ritualised burning of books. It also enabled him to echo the silent films (and by implication those of Hitchcock) he so admired by placing emphasis on the visual. The long, wordless, opening sequence is a good example of this. Foregrounding the image is a nice irony in a film about the importance of literature. There are, too, the familiar observations on relationships: the break-up of one (Linda-Montag) and the formation of another (Clarisse-Montag). But the characters are thinly drawn and the nuanced insights that are Truffaut's forte are conspicuous by their absence. The obsession with books and his parodying of the genre occupy the space normally allotted to social and psychological observation.

Talking about the film in 1970, Truffaut explained how he disliked violence: "For me, what replaces violence is running away, not from what is essential but in order to obtain what is essential. That is what I showed in *Fahrenheit 451*."[45] From childhood, he had avoided confrontation, seeking to achieve his ends by other less direct means. Thus the film is 'an apology for cunning. "OK, so books are banned? Fine, we'll learn them by heart." Now that's cunning.'[46] His passion for books shines through, the notion of 'book people' is intriguing but these features are not enough to make this one of his better films.

Still from 'La Mariée était en noir' (1967)
Julie Kohler (Jeanne Moreau) at the funeral of one of her victims, Fergus.

ABOVE
Still from 'La Mariée était en noir' (1967)
On her wedding day, Julie's husband David
(Serge Rousseau) is shot and killed.

RIGHT
Still from 'La Mariée était en noir' (1967)
Delvaux (Daniel Boulanger) pulled the trigger of
the gun that killed David. He did not know that it
was loaded. The five friends in the room decide
to leave, separate and start new lives.

Still from 'La Mariée était en noir' (1967)
Julie tracks down each of the five men with a view to killing them in revenge. When Julie becomes a model for artist Fergus (Charles Denner), he falls in love with her and paints her on the wall by his bed.

Still from 'La Mariée était en noir' (1967)
Fergus casts Julie as Diana the huntress, unaware that she wants to stop his heart rather than capture it.

The public shunned the film and the Carrosse's finances again came under pressure. Truffaut had to put something together quickly. After David Goodis (*Tirez sur le pianiste*), he turned to another American thriller writer, William Irish (pen name of Cornell Woolrich), and his novel, *The Bride Wore Black,* which now became the focus of another adaptation undertaken by himself and Jean-Louis Richard. De Baecque and Toubiana have defined the nature of Irish's attraction for Truffaut: in his novels the gangsters are relegated to the background while centre stage are ordinary, if highly vulnerable and sensitive, men and women who rush headlong into love and death.[48] The story of *La Mariée était en noir* is a simple one. Julie Kohler's husband is shot and killed on the steps of the church where they have just been married. Although it later transpires that the killing was a grotesque accident, Julie identifies the five men involved and ruthlessly hunts them down, killing each in turn to exact her revenge.

The influence of Hitchcock is particularly strong in *La Mariée était en noir*. There are numerous parallels. Julie Kohler is a heroine despite her brutal murder of five men; we sympathise with her and applaud her on completion of her mission. Structurally, Truffaut deviates from Irish's novel by moving the dénouement to an early point in the film, thus adopting a device employed by Hitchcock in *Vertigo* (1958) and *Psycho* (1960). *La Mariée était en noir* remains a thriller and an exploration of the mechanics of suspense. Not, however, in the traditional 'whodunnit' sense. Once the reason for Julie's actions is revealed, the audience is no longer interested in what caused them, only in how she will execute them. Truffaut, like Hitchcock, was then able to concentrate on creating suspense and tension within each sequence. A third similarity lies in the almost total disregard for realism. Both refused to go to the lengths necessary to ensure that everything was realistic. They had other more important goals. Finally, Truffaut again exploits the genre – this time that of the thriller – for his own ends. The film is only marginally concerned with a murder hunt and the police have a low profile.

Despite varied influences, the structure of 'one versus five' is a familiar one: it was used in *Les Mistons* (couple v. kids) and will recur in *Une belle fille comme moi.* Truffaut uses the device here, somewhat schematically, to portray five males with five different perspectives on women and love: the vain Bliss, the dreamer Coral, the pompous Morane, the brutal Delvaux and the womanising Fergus. They are clearly distinguished from each other but, to varying degrees, are all unfaithful, lecherous, superficial and with stereotypical views of the opposite sex. Julie is another of Truffaut's strong female protagonists, the focus of the action and prompter of the plot. In comparison, the males are again weak, hesitant, immature and easily led into Julie's traps by her exploitation of their foibles. She is, finally, one of the best illustrations of the 'absolutist' stance, pursuing her self-imposed task with a ruthless single-mindedness.

The shooting of *La Mariée était en noir* was punctuated by the death in a car accident of Françoise Dorléac. Truffaut was deeply affected. He was haunted by death; it is a theme present in many of his films, and rose to the surface in *La Chambre verte. La Mariée était en noir* was well received by the public. Truffaut later believed Jeanne Moreau was badly miscast and regretted the film was made in colour, 'which robbed it of all mystery.'[49] He formed the theory that just as some actors were hurt by the transition from silent films to talkies, others were equally damaged by the transition from black and white to colour movies, and he felt that Jeanne Moreau was one of those actors.

On the set of 'La Mariée était en noir' (1967)
Truffaut on the prison set that features at the end of the film.

ABOVE
On the set of 'La Mariée était en noir' (1967)
Filming the close-up of the mysterious woman
(Jeanne Moreau) pushing Bliss off the balcony
to his death and telling him "I'm Julie Kohler."

LEFT
On the set of 'La Mariée était en noir' (1967)
Whilst filming Bliss' engagement party, François
Truffaut makes notes in his script as Jeanne
Moreau, Claude Rich and Jean-Claude Brialy
wait for him.

ABOVE
Still from 'Baisers volés' (1968)
After a caress (see page 22), Antoine Doinel
(Jean-Pierre Léaud) steals a kiss from the prim
and proper Christine Darbon (Claude Jade) in
her parents' wine cellar. Christine will steal a kiss
from him in the wine cellar in 'Domicile
conjugal.' Truffaut links the Doinel films visually
with this kiss by having Christine wear red each
time. See page 110 for 'Domicile conjugal' and
page 22 for 'L'Amour en fuite.'

RIGHT
Still from 'Baisers volés' (1968)
Antoine experiments with different woman and
although his date with a tall woman is visually
amusing he finds it very satisfying sexually. So
much so, in fact, that in 'Domicile conjugal' he
selects a tall prostitute to sleep with.

Still from 'Baisers volés' (1968)
Antoine is somewhat shaken when he meets his
old flame Colette Tazzi (Marie-France Pisier) with
her husband Albert (Jean-François Adam) and
child.

Following two comparatively rigid and detailed scenarios, the one for his next
film, *Baisers volés*, was sketchy and fluid, undergoing late rewrites and with many
improvisations in the shooting. The idea for this, the third Doinel film, had been in
Truffaut's mind for about three years. The choice of crew and cast was quickly
completed in January 1968.

Antoine, now a young man, is discharged from the army before working as a
night porter in an hotel, as an assistant in a private detective agency and then as a
TV repairman. His emotional life is equally haphazard. He frequents prostitutes, is
seduced by an older woman and finally proposes to Christine. The plot line, a
compilation of discrete episodes, resembles those of *Les Mistons* and *Les Quatre
Cents Coups,* which are similarly picaresque. As Truffaut wrote, 'We stuffed the film
full of all sorts of things linked to the theme which Balzac called "a start in life."'[50]
It is not the unfolding of the story that maintains our interest, rather our deepening
understanding of Antoine's character and those of the people who surround him.

Baisers volés might have been put together very quickly, but it still taps rich veins
of inspiration and is thematically varied and multi-layered. If the preceding films
were made mainly under the influence of Hitchcock, *Baisers volés* can be seen as
subscribing to a more Renoirian vision of the world. "People are great," says Mme
Tabard echoing her father's dying words, and many of the characters in the film

Still from 'Baisers volés' (1968)
Antoine gets a job at a hotel but loses it when private investigator Monsieur Henri (Harry-Max) tricks him into letting a husband catch his wife with another man. Monsieur Henri helps the endearing but bumbling Antoine get a job at the Blady Detective Agency.

confirm its largely optimistic and upbeat tone. There is another significant shift, this time in the 'provisional-permanent' dichotomy. The whole film is predicated on the provisional, from its conception to its execution. Little in Antoine's life is permanent, and in work and love he repeatedly, at times bewilderingly, changes tack. Yet the absolute is not entirely excluded. Its presence is embodied in the stranger who stalks Christine for much of the film and who, at the end of the film, finally speaks. He urges Christine to leave Antoine, who can only offer a provisional love, a provisional life, whereas he offers the permanent, the absolute. Truffaut himself only fully came to realise the importance of this scene eight years later when he wrote '[it] is the key to almost all the stories I tell.'[51] The film might end with Antoine's marriage in prospect, but we have little evidence to sustain the belief that it will endure.

Truffaut's complex attitude to women takes further twists here. 'Are women magic?' is a question that male characters ask in several films. Angel or whore? Both 'types' are here. Mme Tabard plays a key role in demythologising woman and making the case for Truffaut as someone who was at least aware of the feminist perspective. She steps down from the pedestal on which Antoine placed her and joins him in bed to share brief but very earthly and most unangelic pleasures. The on-off relationship with Christine, conducted simultaneously with visits to

ABOVE
Still from 'Baisers volés' (1968)
Antoine goes undercover at Georges Tabard's shoe shop to find out why the staff hate Georges. Instead Antoine falls for Monsieur Tabard's worldly and sophisticated wife Fabienne. Here Antoine repeatedly recites Fabienne's name, Christine's name and his own name until he breaks down in exhaustion. It is as if each of the women is exerting control over him and he must establish control of himself.

LEFT
Still from 'Baisers volés' (1968)
When Fabienne Tabard (Delphine Seyrig) receives a love letter from Antoine that has allusions to Honoré de Balzac's 'The Lily in the Valley' (see page 20), she immediately goes to his room and they make love, with the condition that they never see each other again. 'The Lily in the Valley' was a book that Truffaut had read when young, and there are also references to Balzac in 'Les Quatre Cents Coups' (Antoine has a shrine to Balzac which goes up in flames) and 'La Peau douce.'

prostitutes, reflects a more prosaic, day-to-day picture of romance. The Doinel character grows and deepens, with Truffaut giving Léaud free rein to contribute to its creation. Antoine remains, nonetheless, impetuous, naïve, charming, infuriating and seemingly incapable of sticking at anything.

Throughout much of the filming, Truffaut had been campaigning on behalf of Langlois and his Cinémathèque, which had played such a key role in his own development. The campaign had a high profile in the media and presaged the more turbulent events of May 1968. The whole incident tells us a great deal about the subject matter of Truffaut's films. 'Why don't you make political films?' asks a minor character in *La Nuit américaine*. It is evident from Truffaut's 24 films that he does not. For Truffaut, politics and films did not mix: life was more complicated than the black and white scenarios of politics. He told Helen Scott that he came from a generation that was not politically committed[52] and later in an interview for the *Nouvel Observateur* stated 'life is neither Nazi, nor Communist, nor Gaullist, it's anarchic.'[53]

Spring 1968 marked another turbulent period in his life. He had become infatuated with Claude Jade during the filming of *Baisers volés* and came close to marrying her. Connections made in researching private detective agencies for this film led him to seek to establish the identity of his biological father. The enquiry led to Roland Lévy, a dentist from Bayonne now practising in Belfort. He was Jewish. His mother's family disputed the findings of the enquiry but Truffaut believed it explained certain aspects of his character: 'his sympathy for outcasts, martyrs, those living on the fringes of society.'[54] Finally, the emotional upheaval of these events was exacerbated by his mother's death in August 1968. He had still not forgiven her (and vice versa).

On the set of 'Baisers volés' (1968)
The film was dedicated to Henri Langlois (right), the legendary artistic director of the Cinémathèque Française, an independent nonprofit organisation he had founded in 1936 and the place where movie-lovers met. The French Ministry of Cultural Affairs removed him from office on 9 February 1968. Truffaut (who was filming and editing 'Baisers volés') and the New Wave rallied to his defence and mobilised directors from around the world to protest by refusing to allow their films to be shown. Protest marches were held on 12 February and 14 February (when policemen charged and injured the directors and actors), and after many meetings, Langlois was reinstated on 22 April. On 2 May, the film theatre was reopened to an enthusiastic crowd who heard Langlois exclaim "Make way for the movies!"

Against all expectations *Baisers volés* was a financial success. Light-hearted, comic, nostalgic, the film turned its back on France's political and social upheavals, offering the public relief from its misery. Confident after their triumph, Truffaut and the Carrosse turned to their next venture. Like *La Mariée était en noir*, *La Sirène du Mississippi* is adapted from a William Irish novel, *Waltz into Darkness*. The film was partly shot in an exotic – and therefore costly – location (Reunion) and the two lead roles were taken by the then two biggest names in French cinema: Jean-Paul Belmondo and Catherine Deneuve. Both, significantly, had established screen personae.

Louis Mahé and Julie Roussel make contact through the small-ads. Both seek love and a relationship. Julie sails to Reunion to meet the wealthy Louis. They quickly marry. Louis deposits all his money in a joint account. Julie disappears with the money. Her real name is Marion Bergamo and she is working with her lover, Richard. The real Julie Roussel had told her story on the boat and Richard had thrown her overboard so that Marion could take her place. Berthe Roussel, sister of Julie, and Louis hire a private detective, Comolli, to bring Marion to justice. Louis leaves for France. By chance, he finds Marion and, tries to shoot her but he cannot bring himself to pull the trigger. She explains that Richard had taken all the money and left her. Louis and Marion start a new life in a villa near Aix-en-Provence. Comolli meanwhile is hot on her tracks and, literally, bumps into Louis in the street. Knowing that Comolli will charge Marion with the murder of Julie Roussel, Louis kills him and buries the body in the cellar. They flee to Lyon. Comolli's body is found and the story appears in the press. Louis returns to Reunion and sells his

On the set of 'Baisers volés' (1968)
Filming the opening establishing shot. The Eiffel
Tower is a recurring image in Truffaut's films. In
fact, in 1957 he was signed to direct a short film
about a man who can see the Eiffel Tower but
cannot get to it. This was the inspiration for the
opening titles of 'Les Quatre Cents Coups.' The
tower is also on a poster in the opening scene of
'L'Amour en fuite.' Truffaut, whose apartment
had an inspirational view of the monument,
collected Eiffel Tower replicas of all sizes, and
one of these is even used as a weapon in
'Vivement dimanche!' (see poster on page 191).

LEFT
On the set of 'Baisers volés' (1968)
Filming the funeral of Monsieur Henri.

95

ABOVE
Still from 'La Sirène du Mississippi' (1969)
When Louis Mahé (Jean-Paul Belmondo) marries Julie Roussel (Catherine Deneuve) she turns out to be an imposter and robs him of almost 28 million Francs. He pursues her and kills a private eye to protect her. After this act, they make passionate love.

RIGHT
Still from 'La Sirène du Mississippi' (1969)
When Louis catches up with Julie, he wants to kill her. "I'm willing to die," she tells him.

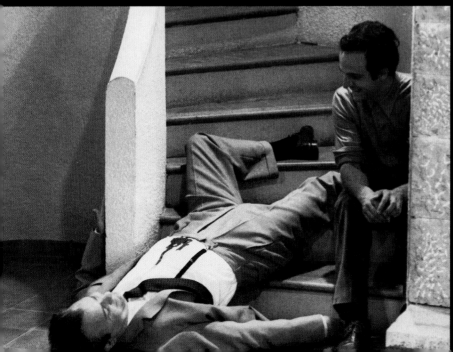

*"All the roles an actor plays contribute to the
creation of a "persona" against which s/he cannot
really struggle. It's better to go along with it."*

François Truffaut [56]

OPPOSITE TOP
Still from 'La Sirène du Mississippi' (1969)
Louis tells Julie that loving her involves both
suffering and joy.

OPPOSITE BOTTOM
Still from 'La Sirène du Mississippi' (1969)
The final scene, where Julie and Louis walk off
towards the border and an unknown future, is
just one of several references to Jean Renoir's
films. The film is dedicated to the great director,
and begins with a clip from 'La Marseillaise.' At
one point Louis plans to see a film called
'Arizona Jim', a reference to the fictional Western
character in 'Le Crime de Monsieur Lange.'

PAGE 100
On the set of 'La Sirène du Mississippi' (1969)
Catherine Deneuve's 'ice blonde' look would
have been perfect for an Alfred Hitchcock
thriller. Louis calls Julie a "parasite who lives
outside normal society."

PAGE 101
On the set of 'La Sirène du Mississippi' (1969)
Deneuve has an opaqueness that means she
can hide her character's real feelings. This is an
ideal quality for a noir romance.

business at half price. Back in France, he hides the money in their flat. They go out, but on their return, the police are searching the building and they have to flee again, this time to a small chalet in the mountains. Marion tries to poison Louis but he realises what she is doing. He tells her he knows but that he still loves and forgives her. Marion breaks down, saying that she is not worthy of such love. Love, Louis says, involves both joy and suffering.

La Sirène du Mississippi is a nuanced exploration of the development of a complicated relationship. Unusually for a Truffaut film, there is no real threat to the couple from a third party. Marion, an orphan, is a prostitute, accomplice to murder and attempts murder. She is streetwise, cynical and seeking material well-being. Louis, in contrast, is naïve, trusting and indifferent to his wealth. The film charts the movement toward a mutual understanding of these individuals from two disparate worlds. The ending is delightfully ambiguous: the degree to which Louis might have lost his unworldliness and Marion might have come to trust Louis is not resolved, a position underlined at the close of the film by the allusion to Renoir's *La Grande Illusion* (1937). Louis and Marion, like Maréchal and Rosenthal before them, wander off into the snowbound, featureless landscape, their destination and future unknown.

The film constitutes the clearest statement yet of the theme of the provisional and the absolute. Louis tells Marion what he believed he and Julie Roussel had been seeking in their letters: 'We were looking to establish something permanent, but instead you came, bringing me the provisional.' As his love for Marion grows, overcoming his keen desire for revenge, it becomes pure, blind, absolute, accepting even her attempt to poison him. In the face of this unswerving and unselfish passion, Marion crumbles and accepts that her destiny is bound to his, for the time being at least. *La Sirène du Mississippi* marks another staging post in Truffaut's continual wrestling with the notion of the couple. A *modus vivendi* appears to have been wrought and from the most unlikely characters and circumstances. Or has it? Does the last scene, with its reference to *La Grande Illusion*, suggest that the 'grand illusion' is love itself?

The film was another – relative – failure. Truffaut attributed this in part to the casting of Belmondo and Deneuve against their established screen personae. The audiences could not accept an 'innocent' Belmondo any more than they could believe in a 'corrupt' Deneuve. The shooting of *La Sirène du Mississippi* had for its director been a happy if highly charged experience. He had again fallen in love with his 'leading lady.'

The idea for his next film, *L'Enfant sauvage,* had existed for some time and Jean Gruault had written a first scenario as early as 1965. Truffaut's longstanding interest in the well-being and protection of children sprang from his own experience. He continued to work on the project, researching carefully and watching films on relevant topics. As usual, financing was not easy – in the end United Artists were persuaded to provide the money. The crew underwent few changes, the notable exception being that the role of cameraman was taken by Nestor Almendros, well known for his work with Rohmer. This was the first of nine films Almendros would make with Truffaut and the start of a highly productive professional and personal relationship. Shooting began in early July 1969 and was completed by the end of August.

The story, a true one, is based on two medical reports by Dr Jean Itard. The first, written in 1801, is scientific in tone and purpose, the second, dating from 1806, is a bid for a grant. Truffaut remains largely faithful to these texts. In 1798, a young boy aged about ten is chased and captured by hunters in woods in the Aveyron. At the instigation of Dr Itard, the child – apparently a deaf-mute – is brought to Paris, initially to the National Institute for the Deaf and Dumb. The doctors quickly determine that an attempt had been made to slit the child's throat and that he had probably been abandoned, presumed dead. As he makes no progress at the Institute, Dr Pinel suggests he is retarded and that he be moved to a mental home. Itard succeeds in having the boy transferred to his own home where he is cared for by Mme Guérin. The second half of the film concentrates principally on Itard's attempt to educate the boy. He gives him a name – Victor – and teaches him to walk, dress, sleep, eat and live like others. In particular, he tries to teach him to talk and communicate. Progress is difficult and slow. One day, Victor flees. The film ends with his return to Dr Itard.

L'Enfant sauvage is perhaps the closest Truffaut comes to making a committed film. Few causes ever prompted Truffaut to take direct action: the protection of children was, however, one of them. In its exclusive focus on Victor, it has a strong documentary feel, accentuated by the director's return to black and white and the grainy texture of Almendros' photography. Although Truffaut was attracted by Itard's literary – even poetic – style, the film is not really fictional; it follows real events and characters very closely. These factors combine to make *L'Enfant sauvage* a polemical film, its director seeking to arouse awareness and stimulate debate around the subject of abused children. At its heart is a well-manipulated tension arising from the dual nature of modern, civilised society. On the one hand lie the positive forces of education and Victor's slow but sure progress; on the other, the cruel, perverse behaviour of so-called civilised people. The child is pursued by hunters far more barbaric than himself, taunted by peasants who mock his animal-like appearance and gait, and gawped at by wealthy Parisians who pay to see the latest curiosity, like an exhibit at a fair. Even a highly educated doctor quickly comes to categorise the boy as an 'idiot' fit only for the asylum. Little surprise, then, that the film's most convincing scene is that in which Itard unjustly punishes Victor in an attempt to determine whether or not he has developed a sense of right and wrong.

In one way, the film marked a turning point for Truffaut. For the first time, he played the father, thus facing some of the dilemmas of the role. The film is dedicated to Léaud and, although the wild child is played by another Jean-Pierre, there can be no mistaking that the wild child was, in reality, the troublesome star of *Les Quatre Cents Coups*, and thus Truffaut himself.

"It would be absolutely impossible for me [to make a 'committed' film] since I am the personification of non-commitment and since the spirit of contradiction is deeply rooted in me."

François Truffaut [58]

Publicity still for 'L'Enfant sauvage' (1969)
In an effort to escape, Victor (Jean-Pierre Cargol) breaks a window with his head.

ABOVE
Still from 'L'Enfant sauvage' (1969)
At the beginning of the film, Victor is hunted
down like an animal.

RIGHT
Still from 'L'Enfant sauvage' (1969)
Dr Itard (François Truffaut) looks after Victor to
"examine the degree of intelligence of a child
devoid of education." In one experiment, he
punishes the boy unjustly and Victor revolts
against it by biting Dr Itard. 'The bite filled me
with joy,' the doctor remarks, because it showed
that the boy knew right from wrong.

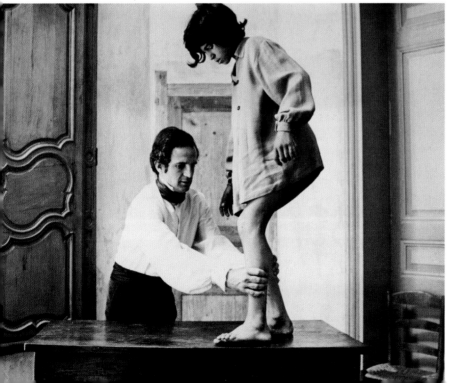

ABOVE
Still from 'L'Enfant sauvage' (1969)
When Victor first saw a flame he was frightened
of it. Later, he is inquisitive about it.

LEFT
Still from 'L'Enfant sauvage' (1969)
Dr Itard teaches Victor how to walk upright.
Notice the calluses on Victor's knees from
walking on four limbs.

The film was generally well received and had a modest success at the box office, offsetting the disappointing financial performance of *La Sirène du Mississippi*. Although he argued that it was the nature of the role, Truffaut does not convince as Itard: his performance is wooden and lacking in nuance. The subject matter is rather too often close to the mechanics of pedagogy; it is technical and devoid of humour and dramatic incident. Despite its taut structure, an impressive performance by Jean-Pierre Cargol, cogent use of imagery (e.g. windows and doors) and a striking contribution from Almendros, *L'Enfant sauvage* is not one of Truffaut's better films.

The film was financially successful and restored the fortunes of the Films du Carrosse. Truffaut's relationship with Catherine Deneuve had brought happiness and stability. His health was good. The decade was ending on a positive note and Truffaut could face the future with renewed confidence. Sadly, these good times were to prove 'provisional.'

BELOW & OPPOSITE
On the set of 'L'Enfant sauvage' (1969)
François Truffaut draws out a magnificent performance from Jean-Pierre Cargol by spending a lot of time with him.

Victor lives happily outside 'civilisation' and only becomes unhappy when he is brought into civilisation and prevented from drinking pure water, or walking through the woods, or feeling rain on his face, or dancing under the moon. In the end, after escaping, Victor returns to Dr Itard because he no longer has the senses he needs to survive in the wild. Victor's last, long, hard look at Dr Itard is an accusation that a grave injustice has been done. Now Victor is trapped in civilisation.

Let Cinema Reign!
1970–1976

At the beginning of the 1970s, Truffaut's reputation was secure. At home, he had become a celebrated director, with major interviews and frequent appearances on TV. For his next project, he returned to Antoine Doinel with the idea of completing the cycle. The budget was modest and the flat above the Carrosse offices served as the young couple's home.

The storyline is relatively uncomplicated. Antoine is now married to Christine, working as a flower seller but in fact experimenting with dyes to produce an 'Absolute Red' carnation. We enter the couple's daily routine: Christine works as a violin teacher whilst Antoine is in the courtyard with his dyes and flowers. There are meals with her parents, conversations in bed and encounters with the varied and numerous characters who inhabit the same block of flats. There is much laughter and they appear happy. Christine becomes pregnant and Alphonse is born. Having failed to produce his 'Absolute Red,' Antoine successfully applies for a job with an American hydraulics company. There he meets the beautiful Kyoko. They begin an affair. By chance, Christine receives notes from Kyoko intended for Antoine. She reacts angrily and Antoine leaves her and moves in with Kyoko. He rapidly tires of her. Kyoko dumps him. A year later, Antoine and Christine are back together.

On the surface, *Domicile conjugal* is a slight and inconsequential film, humorous, optimistic and cheerful. As with the earlier Doinel films, the scenario is primarily Truffaut's, packed with observations on social behaviour, language, characters both 'normal' and eccentric, ways of living, and all no doubt taken from notes he had compiled over years and from his colleagues and friends. There are 'gags,' one-liners and allusions, such as the gratuitous 'Jacques Tati' sequence in the metro station. The array of minor characters is quite breathtaking in its diversity: the opera singer and his wife in the flat next door, the concierge, the cafe owner, his customers, the raunchy waitress, the man who won't leave his flat, the young man living alone, the prostitute and the scrounging friend.

Closer analysis reveals a different picture. The film is structured around contrasting approaches to love and relationships. At the centre are Antoine and Christine, lurching from laughter to argument, living the day-to-day tensions of life in a small flat, bringing up a child, finding and keeping a job. The film amounts to the anatomy of a marriage, and charts its slow disintegration. It is in somewhat

Still from 'La Nuit américaine' (1973)
François Truffaut plays the director Ferrand in the filming of the film 'Meet Pamela' within the film. The name Ferrand is a shortening of Truffaut's mother's maiden name Monferrand. He has a hearing aid in his left ear, which is a reference to the hearing difficulty Truffaut acquired whilst in the French army.

"The art of film can only really exist through a highly organised betrayal of reality."
François Truffaut [59]

desultory fashion that Antoine takes his Japanese mistress. "I am never bored," he shouts at Christine. Yet by the end of the film he is phoning his wife three times from the restaurant where he is dining with Kyoko to complain of the crushing boredom he is experiencing with her. With an irony that escapes him, he begins to woo his wife while in the company of his mistress. Antoine is as confused as ever, telling Christine that she is his little sister, his daughter, his mother. Poignantly she replies, "But all I wanted was to be your wife!" Christine is dignified, mature, and responsible in a way that Antoine will never be. The film must have been hurtful for Madeleine, though the contrast between the impetuous and shallow Antoine/Truffaut and the patient, perceptive Christine/Madeleine may have offset her pain.

Literally juxtaposed with this young couple are their neighbours, the middle-aged opera singer and his wife. Time sharpens rather than blunts the tensions. In the last scene of the film Antoine, impatiently waiting for his wife, throws her hat and coat down the stairs just as the opera singer had done earlier. Living as a couple means coming to terms with the mundane irritations of familiarity. Minor characters represent other approaches to love. Antoine's visit to the prostitute is here presented sympathetically. The waitress Jeannette repeatedly seeks to seduce a perplexed Antoine. The mysterious 'Strangler,' a young man living alone, quickly becomes the centre of a web of rumour and innuendo. The man who will not leave his flat has opted out of meaningful relationships and spends his life at his window or in front of his TV, living vicariously.

At the hub of this many-spoked wheel is Antoine, grown up but not grown up, as his new job manoeuvring 'toy' boats in a miniature port underlines. He still has no fixed purpose in life, still moves from one form of employment to another, motivated more by whim than resolve. The gap between his ambitions and reality is as wide as ever: he sells carnations but dreams of creating new colours; frustrated, he gives up and changes job but all the time sees himself as a writer. His work with flowers and dyes is a cogent metaphor for his character. He is striving to create an 'Absolute Red.' The catastrophic outcome of his experiment, the smoking, devastated flowers, graphically demonstrates his failure to attain the absolute: Antoine will forever remain the epitome of the 'provisional' man.

In its concentration on multiple relationships, the repeated use of deep focus and in its setting, *Domicile conjugal* represents Truffaut's most overt homage to Jean Renoir. The courtyard is unmistakably a reference to Renoir's *Le Crime de Monsieur Lange* (1936) and draws us into a similar complex of intertwined lives and relationships. The positive features of communal life in a Parisian apartment block with their open doors, open windows, shared lives and rich colloquial language sustain both films.

The film was released on 9 September 1970 and was an instant success, as had been *L'Enfant sauvage* before it. The Carrosse was rolling again and normally Truffaut would have turned to his next project with renewed enthusiasm and confidence. Circumstances, sadly, were not normal. Making four films in just over two years had left him physically and mentally exhausted. This, combined with the breakup of his relationship with Catherine Deneuve, led to a severe depression.

One of the spurs to recovery was Henri-Pierre Roché's second novel *Les Deux Anglaises et le Continent*. Truffaut's response to disappointment in love was work. He had begun negotiations with Gallimard for rights to the book as early as 1968 and Jean Gruault had been working on a scenario, reading not only the novel but

ABOVE
Still from 'Domicile conjugal' (1970)
Antoine Doinel (Jean-Pierre Léaud) and Christine (Claude Jade) are now a married couple. This kiss echoes their first one (see page 90).

OPPOSITE TOP
Still from 'Domicile conjugal' (1970)
Truffaut often signals future events and underlying tensions with unexplained actions and props. In the opening scene, it is established that Christine is married (because she insists upon being called "Madame" not "Mademoiselle"), and also that she is interested in the Russian dancer Nureyev. Does she want a man like him rather than the childish Antoine? Antoine is interested in Kyoko, the Japanese woman he met at work, so he researches this exotic new world.

OPPOSITE BOTTOM
Still from 'Domicile conjugal' (1970)
Christine finds out that Antoine has been cheating on her with Kyoko. He returns home to find her dressed as a Japanese woman.

TOP
Still from 'Domicile conjugal' (1970)
Antoine says that Christine could name her breasts. For example, Laurel and Hardy.

ABOVE
Still from 'Domicile conjugal' (1970)
Antoine always falls in love with the parents (Claire Duhamel and Daniel Ceccaldi) as well as the girl. In this case, the parents are unaware of the marital problems of the young couple.

LEFT
Still from 'Domicile conjugal' (1970)
Antoine still lives in the apartment but sleeps in another room on a mattress. He spends all his time writing an autobiographical novel, which is published as 'Les Salades de l'amour' between this film and 'L'Amour en fuite' (see page 163).

On the set of 'Domicile conjugal' (1970)
François Truffaut and Jean-Pierre Léaud had a
long and fruitful relationship that extended
beyond their films together. They would meet
often, and he asked François' opinion about
every project he was offered.

On the set of 'Domicile conjugal' (1970)
Antoine touches his newborn baby tentatively on
the head, as a young child might touch a new
member of the family, or like a father discovering
he now has a responsibility towards a fragile
being.

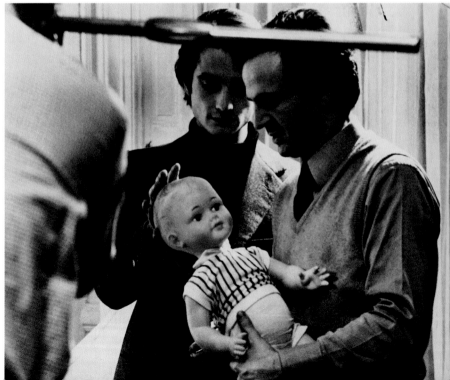

114

ABOVE
Still from 'Domicile conjugal' (1970)
Antoine has dinner with Kyoko (Hiroko Berghauer) at her apartment. He finds it somewhat uncomfortable and has problems with his blood circulation.

LEFT
On the set of 'Domicile conjugal' (1970)
Truffaut gives Léaud an idea of how to play the scene.

**Still from 'Les Deux Anglaises et le Continent'
(1971)**
After falling in love with Muriel Brown and failing
to remain in love with her for the duration of a
trial separation, Claude Roc (Jean-Pierre Léaud)
has a relationship with her free-spirited sister
Anne (Kika Markham).

*"Half of my films are romantic, the others strive to
destroy romance."*

François Truffaut [60]

also Roché's voluminous diary. The film which resulted combined material from
both these sources with unused material from *Jules et Jim*. Éva and Laura –
Truffaut's daughters – feature in the opening credits sequence. The Cotentin
peninsula in Normandy was chosen to substitute for Wales. For other scenes not
set in Paris, locations were found in the Jura and the Ardèche (for the sequences
involving the train).

The story begins at the start of the twentieth century. Claude Roc is from a
wealthy family. Brought up in Paris by his mother – his father died when he was
young – he is interested in the arts and literature. He meets Anne Brown, a
sculptress and the daughter of an English friend of his mother. Shortly afterwards
he makes a lengthy visit to the Browns in their seaside home in Wales. Anne
repeatedly encourages Claude to take an interest in Muriel, her sister. Claude
declares his love to Muriel who, after initially giving him no hope, abruptly changes
her mind. Mme Roc travels from Paris. She is opposed to a marriage. A
compromise is reached: Claude will leave and the couple will not communicate for
a year. If their feelings for each other are unchanged neither family would stand in
the way of a union. Claude returns to Paris, takes lovers and after several months
writes to Muriel breaking off the relationship. Although she replies nonchalantly,
Muriel is in fact heartbroken. Anne comes to Paris and takes a studio. She and
Claude have an affair. Muriel comes to Paris and tells Claude she still loves him. He
returns this love but Anne and he decide she must know of their affair. Anne tells
Muriel, who flees. It is Claude's turn to be heartbroken and he becomes depressed,

writing a novel, *Jerome and Julian*, as a way of overcoming his grief. Anne dies of tuberculosis. Muriel passes through Calais on her way to take up a teaching post in Brussels. Claude meets her and they spend a night together before parting for good.

Truffaut was pleased with *Les Deux Anglaises et le Continent*, believing it to be one of his best films to date. Not all the critics agreed and it received mixed reviews. If *Domicile conjugal* corresponds to most people's ideas of the typical Truffaut film, *Les Deux Anglaises et le Continent* is the opposite. That this film is to be different in subject and tone is made explicit in the opening sequence. In contrast to *Domicile conjugal*, which was regularly punctuated with shots of women's legs ascending stairs, we here see a man coming down the stairs, on crutches. What is more, though we may recognise Léaud, he is clearly not playing Antoine Doinel whose dashing to and fro is in sharp contrast to this slow descent.

The film is unsatisfactory from a number of points of view. In order, he claimed, to help Léaud shed his Doinel persona, Truffaut took a considerable risk in casting him as Claude Roc, a wealthy, bourgeois aesthete. This barely works. Léaud fails to convince as Claude. His performance is wooden, too deliberate. The aura of Doinel is not dispelled. The film is sombre and serious in mood throughout, and totally devoid of humour. Truffaut acknowledged that 'the story was so romantic, possibly even melodramatic, that it had to be balanced by some very physical scenes'[61] and it does indeed lurch from the intensely (melo)dramatic to the starkly physical. Truffaut wrote, 'Rather than a film about physical love, I have tried to make a physical film about love.'[62] Many have commented on the most blatant example of

Still from 'Les Deux Anglaises et le Continent' (1971)
Claude is fascinated by the intense and enigmatic Muriel Brown (Stacey Tendeter). They only have brief moments together, which only heightens the sexual tension between them.

ABOVE
Still from 'Les Deux Anglaises et le Continent' (1971)
Sheltering from the rain, Claude is placed between Muriel and Anne as they rock back and forth singing a song. Mrs Brown (Sylvia Marriott, right) laughs at the innocence of the song, but Claude can feel the bodies of the young women rubbing against him.

LEFT
On the set of 'Les Deux Anglaises et le Continent' (1971)
Truffaut checks the composition.

PAGES 120/121
On the set of 'Les Deux Anglaises et le Continent' (1971)
When Claude must leave for a trial separation from Muriel, we see the women from Claude's point of view. Here Truffaut and his crew take the shot whilst hanging from the train.

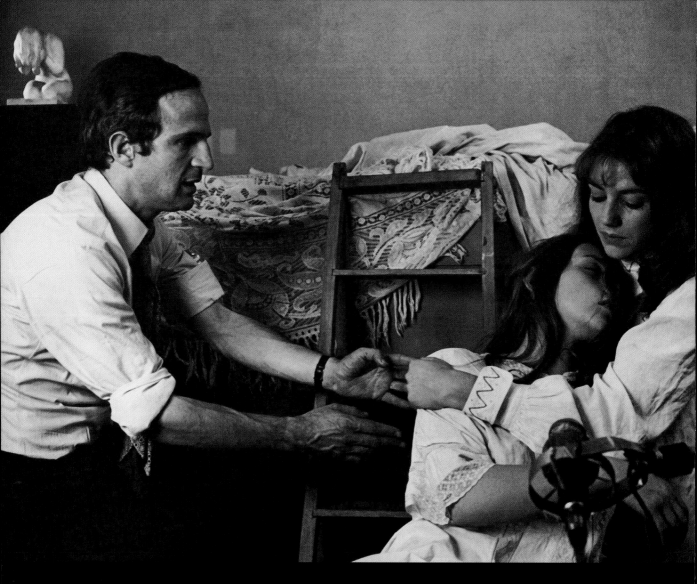

this: the camera's lingering on the bloodstained sheets following the deflowering of
Muriel at the end of the film. These abrupt changes in tone – from the romantic to
the physical – disturb rather than enlighten the spectator. The film is suffused with
an exaggerated Romanticism that is due in part at least to Truffaut's identifying
similarities with the Brontë sisters about whom he read a great deal in preparing the
film. Anne Brown's death is modelled on that of Emily, whose dying words, 'My
mouth is full of dirt', Anne repeats.

The film was released in November 1971 and did not do well in Paris, though it
was reasonably successful abroad. Truffaut's depression had begun to lift: in part
because he enjoyed making the film and believed it to be good and in part since he
found consolation in a brief affair with Kika Markham. But perhaps above all,
because of the support he received from the remarkable Madeleine and his two
young daughters, whose company was a sure source of laughter and happiness.
Scarcely pausing for breath, Truffaut turned to his next project, again one that had
been in the pipeline for some time. He had read the novel on which it is based –
Such a Gorgeous Kid Like Me by the American writer Henry Farrell – as early as
November 1969.

The plot is complex, with many twists and turns. The story opens in a library where a woman is looking for a book entitled *Women Criminals* by Stanislas Prévine. She is informed that although it is announced in a catalogue, the book had not been published. Using multiple flashbacks, the film explains why. Prévine, a social scientist, researching for his book, visits Camille Bliss, who is in prison for murder. In a series of taped interviews, she recounts her life story.

Having engineered the death of her own father, she is sent to a detention centre from where she escapes. She marries Clovis Bliss and robs his mother. She and Clovis find work at the Colt Saloon. There she has a liaison with the singer, Sam Golden. Clovis finds out and, going berserk, gets run over. In the confusion, Camille hides in the van of pest-controller, Arthur, a Catholic and sinner whom she later seduces. She takes up with the lawyer Murène who cheats her. Camille attempts to poison Clovis and Murène with Arthur's fumigation machine but Arthur saves their lives. To pay for this, the greatest sin, he insists they commit a double suicide by throwing themselves off the cathedral tower. He jumps to his death, but alone. Camille is found guilty of Arthur's murder. Prévine, who is by now hopelessly in love with her, succeeds in proving her innocence. As Stanislas is about to realise his dream of sleeping with Camille, Clovis bursts in to say his mother has died, leaving a small fortune. He is enraged to find Camille in bed with Stanislas and beats the latter unconscious. Camille shoots Clovis and places the gun in the hand of the still dormant Stanislas. The latter is charged with Clovis' murder and imprisoned. Armed with Isobel Bliss' wealth, Camille becomes the successful cabaret star she had always dreamed of being. She visits Stanislas in prison but ignores his pleas to save him. He sees her on TV about to marry his lawyer and build a swimming pool on the site of the Bliss property where she had engineered the death of Isobel Bliss.

Une belle fille comme moi appears on first viewing to be a light-hearted response to the dark and humourless *Les Deux Anglaises et le Continent*. Truffaut claimed he wanted a change from Roché's measured literary style, and that he had found it in Camille Bliss' colloquial, earthy discourse. He sought also to kill off once and for all the notion of romantic love, of the ideal couple living forever in marital bliss. He had attempted to do this in *Les Deux Anglaises et le Continent* by puncturing the exaggeratedly emotional with the starkly physical. Now, in his next project, he was returning to the attack, this time by demonstrating its absurdity. He illustrates this in the person of Stanislas, whose gullibility and romantic illusions assume almost tragic dimensions, but also through Sam Golden and Murène with their cynical and egotistical take on love. But above all with Camille herself, who ruthlessly exploits her lovers for personal gain before bumping them off or setting them up for crimes she herself committed.

Une belle fille comme moi is richly comic on several levels: it often descends into uproarious farce, the dialogue is frequently very funny and both characters and situation are sources of laughter. And the pace is literally breathtaking. In no sense can this be considered a realist film. The plot twists are implausible and the characters cartoon-like in their exaggeration: Camille, with her vibrant language and natural exuberance, is simply larger than life while Stanislas is gullible beyond the bounds of credibility. An unambiguous sign of this disregard for realism and an indication that the film's significance lies elsewhere is to be found in the early shot in which the young Camille flies through the air to land on top of a haystack, despatched by the boot of her angry and drunken father.

"You can do your utmost to control what you want in a film, but there will always be an important element that completely escapes you."

François Truffaut [63]

ABOVE
Still from 'Une belle fille comme moi' (1972)
In this black comedy, Camille Bliss (Bernadette Lafont) is tricked into signing compromising documents by lawyer Maître Murène (Claude Brasseur).

OPPOSITE TOP
Still from 'Une belle fille comme moi' (1972)
The film rests on Bernadette Lafont's performance as 'female thug' Camille Bliss. Like Julie Roussel in 'La Sirène du Mississippi,' Camille wants money and is willing to do anything to get it.

OPPOSITE BOTTOM
Still from 'Une belle fille comme moi' (1972)
Camille dreams of becoming a nightclub singer and sleeps with singer Sam Golden (Guy Marchand). At the end of the film, even though she has murdered and schemed, Camille becomes a successful singer.

ABOVE
Still from 'Une belle fille comme moi' (1972)
Camille tries to kill husband Clovis Bliss (Philippe Léotard, right) and Murène with a machine that exterminates rats.

RIGHT
Still from 'Une belle fille comme moi' (1972)
Camille hooks up with Arthur (Charles Denner), a mystical rat exterminator who loses his virginity to her and says they should commit suicide together from a church tower. When he jumps alone, Camille is accused of murder and goes to jail.

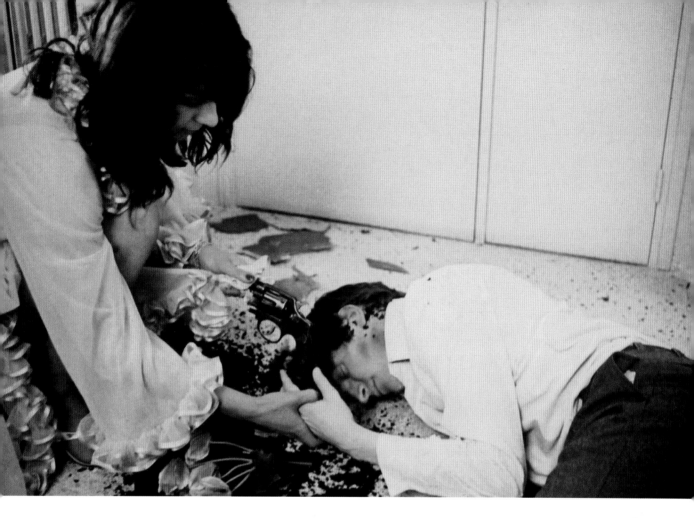

The film is suffused with the energy and vitality of Bernadette Lafont. She is another in Truffaut's line of strong female characters and in this film she manipulates all the main levers of the plot. So powerful is the character that she and Truffaut create that the audience readily sympathises with this completely amoral murderess. In achieving this identification of the audience with Camille, Truffaut was knowingly following in the footsteps of Hitchcock.

On completion of *Une belle fille comme moi*, Truffaut acknowledged that this was Bernadette's film.[64] At the same time, he must have realised that Camille was a female version of Doinel, and thus of himself. Fatherless from an early age, committed to a detention centre, running everywhere, opportunist on a grand scale – these are just some of the obvious similarities. 'I deride [someone like Stanislas] who stubbornly persists in seeing life through rose-tinted glasses and agree with [Camille] who is a kind of hooligan, who has learned to trust no one and to fight for her own survival.'[65]

Sadly, the film did not appeal either to the public or to the critics. Both failed to appreciate its depth and humour. Truffaut ascribed this to his disregard for the rules of the genre (here comedy). He disorients the spectator, who does not know how to react. But it is precisely this subversion of genre, along with the film's solid internal logic and its ability to convey serious messages through the popular medium of comedy, that makes *Une belle fille comme moi* one of Truffaut's most satisfying films.

ABOVE
Still from 'Une belle fille comme moi' (1972)
Camille kills Clovis and frames the sociologist who rescued her from prison, Stanislas Prévine (André Dussolier). He ends up in jail.

PAGES 128/129
On the set of 'Une belle fille comme moi' (1972)
Filming took place mainly in Béziers, but also in Sète and Lunel. In the evening Truffaut often invited the actors to his rented apartment for dinner and enjoyed listening to their jokes. Bernadette Lafont recalled that, "Twice I saw François laugh so hard that he had to leave the table to go throw up."

Still from 'La Nuit américaine' (1973)
Throughout the film, director François Truffaut
(who also plays the director Ferrand), mixes the
reality of the characters with the imaginary film
being made. But it is a double game, because
we are watching a film about a film.

On the set of 'La Nuit américaine' (1973)
This is director François Truffaut rehearsing
Jacqueline Bisset kissing Jean-Pierre Léaud at
the end of the film. (Note the brown leather
jacket that Truffaut often wore (see page 151),
usually with a blue shirt (see pages 144,
182/183). Morane wears a similar jacket in
'L'Homme qui aimait les femmes' (see pages
150, 154 & 155), and Antoine wears both the
jacket and shirt in 'L'Amour en fuite' (see pages
162 & 163).)

Although he was again in danger of working at too fast a pace, Truffaut
immediately plunged into his next film. He had always planned to make a film
about film-making and thought of it every time he made a film 'for the very simple
reason that incredible things happen when you shoot a film, funny, odd, curious
things which the public don't get to know about because they take place off-
screen.'[66] While editing *Les Deux Anglaises et le Continent* at the film studios in
Nice, he noticed an old set and felt it could be renovated for his film about film. He
began work on a scenario with Jean-Louis Richard in the summer of 1971 and
returned to it in January 1972, now with the additional help of Suzanne Schiffman,
who thus contributed to a scenario for the first time. Shooting began at the
Victorine Studios in Nice on 26 September 1972.

La Nuit américaine (the title refers to the technique used to shoot night scenes
in daytime using special filters) is a film about the making of *Meet Pamela*. On one
level, we see the diverse components of film-making: scriptwriting, production,
direction, acting, camerawork, lighting, sound, continuity, music and score. On

La Nuit américaine is another Truffaut film where the main theme is love. On this occasion, although both heterosexual and homosexual love are explored with the now familiar acuteness of observation, the primary focus is a love of cinema. Truffaut often pondered whether cinema was more important than life, and this film provides one answer. In the oft-cited conversation between Ferrand the director and Alphonse, the former states fervently, "Films are more harmonious than life. There are no bottlenecks in films, no times when nothing seems to happen." As Julie Baker, the star, is heard to say through her tears, and as numerous incidents in the film unambiguously demonstrate, "Life is disgusting." It is imperfect, repetitive, at times boring, contradictory, confusing and often filled with suffering and pain. Film, on the other hand, is capable of overcoming all of these. It can manipulate time, overcome boredom, give shape and purpose to life. It can mend broken relationships. Love of cinema is everywhere: crew members stopping to participate in a TV cinema quiz programme, a jokey reference to westerns (the 'wagon train'), the allusion to Renoir's *La Règle du jeu* (*The Rules of the Game*, 1939), Ferrand's package of books on film directors, Julie sleeping with Alphonse in an attempt to ensure he does not quit the film. This love of cinema permeates the whole film and culminates in Joëlle's dismissive judgement of Liliane who leaves the film with the stuntman, "I could leave a bloke for a film but I could never quit a film for a bloke."

Film is immensely powerful, able to create illusions and mislead the spectator. In the first sequence we believe we are watching a scene in a Paris square, only for this

belief to be shattered by cries of "cut" as the camera pulls back to reveal the sets, cameras and crew. Film can even overcome death. Alexandre is killed in a car crash but minutes later appears, 'alive,' in the rushes. Julie (in the form of a stunt double) is killed as her car plunges into a gorge. With the aid of the moviola (an instantaneous playback machine), the action (and time) is reversed and car and driver are made whole again. Film can confer immortality. Actors live on through film. In the perpetual struggle in Truffaut's films between the permanent and the provisional, *La Nuit américaine* makes a key statement: art, the creative act – in Truffaut's case the creation of films – is a means of attaining the absolute, the permanent. Life, in comparison, is temporary, provisional.

Truffaut claimed he only came to realise as he worked on editing the film the extent to which 'All the conflicts in *La Nuit américaine* and [*Meet*] *Pamela* concern problems of identity and paternity.… From the supporting actress Stacey who is pregnant, we know not by whom, to the actress Julie Baker who [in her life] married a doctor old enough to be her father and who [in the film] runs off with her stepfather, to Léaud who kills his father, to Valentina Cortese who drinks because her son has leukaemia.'[67] One might add to Truffaut's list Alexandre who is planning to adopt Christian. Years after the events which generated them, Truffaut's subconscious is apparently still wrestling with deeply personal questions.

The film recovered from a fairly slow start in Paris after it had been very well received, outside the competition, at Cannes. It went on to become one of his most successful films, critically and financially, winning him an Oscar for Best Foreign Film in 1974. Earlier he had been voted Best Director by the New York Film Critics Circle.

ABOVE
Still from 'La Nuit américaine' (1973)
The director Ferrand has a recurring nightmare, which is revealed to be a guilty secret: as a boy he stole 'Citizen Kane' stills from a cinema. As a boy Truffaut also stole film stills.

BELOW
On the set of 'La Nuit américaine' (1973)
When actress Stacey (Alexandra Stewart) is reluctant to wear a swimming costume for her role, it is Ferrand (François Truffaut) who persuades her to continue. She is pregnant, but the footage is edited to hide it.

Still from 'La Nuit américaine' (1973)
The film is fascinating because it reveals a lot of tricks, whether it is a hollow candle fitted with a light to illuminate the actors' faces, or the fake window shown above.

Still from 'L'Histoire d'Adèle H.' (1975)
Adèle Hugo (Isabelle Adjani, right) is obsessed with Lieutenant Pinson (Bruce Robinson). When he refuses to have anything to do with her, she gives him money to pay off his gambling debts and even pays for a prostitute for him. "You're pathetic," he tells her.

"[Isabelle Adjani] is the only actress I know who made me cry in front of a TV screen and, because of that, I wanted to shoot a film with her, very quickly, as soon as possible."

François Truffaut [68]

He took a 'sabbatical' lasting almost two years until funds at the Carrosse were once again running low. As always he had several possible projects to which he could turn. Among them was the *Le Journal d'Adèle Hugo*, edited by an American academic, Frances Guille. This autobiographical account of the life of Victor Hugo's second daughter appealed to him on several fronts. There were a number of hurdles to be cleared: securing the rights proved difficult; the story did not appeal to backers; and Truffaut set his heart on having the 19-year-old Isabelle Adjani in the eponymous role. Frances Guille was eventually won over, at a price. Berbert turned successfully to former partners United Artists. Adjani was contracted to the *Comédie Française* but such was Truffaut's pressure on her that she took an enormous risk and broke her contract.

An innovative feature of the production was the use of music by Maurice Jaubert, a composer of film scores from the Golden Age of French cinema, renowned for his work on films such as Jean Vigo's *L'Atalante* (1934). As so often in Truffaut's films, the score has two tones: on this occasion, jangling and discordant to reflect the heroine's mental state, poignant and lyrical (from a saxophone) to capture the pathos of her descent into madness. Shooting began in Guernsey in early January 1975 and lasted two months. The sequences purportedly in Barbados were shot on a small island off Dakar.

On the set of 'L'Histoire d'Adèle H.' (1975)
A lot of the film is focused on the face of Isabelle Adjani, who recites Adèle's letters and journal aloud. She conveys the mad love that her character feels. Adèle cannot control herself. As she says, "Do you think people are in control of their feelings?"

Léopoldine, the tragic victim of a drowning accident. She even had to share her first name with her mother. She in part sought to establish her identity through writing: her diary and the music album she refers to in letters to her father. In a final desperate attempt to remove the weight of paternity from herself, she repeats over and over as if to erase his existence from her mind, "I am born of an unknown father, of an unknown father, of a totally unknown father."

The theme of love, central to most of Truffaut's films, receives a different inflection in *L'Histoire d'Adèle H*. Having explored the couple, the triangle and even more complicated relationships, Truffaut here films a love story involving just one character.[70] Adèle's love is an obsession, a case of 'amour fou.' The obsession leads inevitably to mental breakdown as she is forced into ever more distorted visions of her life and relationship with Pinson. Despite the exclusive focus on Adèle, one senses that the depiction of mental disorder is not as well-informed as it might have been and is restricted mainly to restless nightmares, wrestling with her own prose and an increasingly dense tissue of lies. Adèle is the latest in the line of Truffaut characters seeking an absolute. The strength of the obsession in this case is such that it shakes loose her grasp on sanity. Again, we conclude, as Truffaut intended, that the 'provisional' offers a more realistic approach to life.

The narrative is driven almost entirely by written communication. There are letters from Adèle to her parents, from Adèle to Pinson, from Hugo to his daughter, from Mrs Baa to Hugo. The diary itself, constantly present, gives us insight

into, and in terms of narration often prompts, Adèle's thoughts and actions. And this frenzy of writing is portrayed physically on the screen: the reams of paper she buys at the bookstore, Adèle's quill, the *poste restante* in Halifax, the letters from her father and the vivid red of their seals. Rarely was the theme of writing and (mis)communication more central to a Truffaut film.

The film was well received, particularly abroad, largely because of media interest in its star. Before it premiered in October 1975, Truffaut was already working on *L'Argent de poche*, his next project.

On the set of 'L'Histoire d'Adèle H.' (1975)
François Truffaut has a short, wordless cameo as an officer whom Adèle mistakes for Lieutenant Pinson.

ABOVE
Still from 'L'Argent de poche' (1976)
In an incredible story, little Grégory climbs out of a high window and falls to the ground, but is unhurt. Throughout the film, Truffaut shows the resilience of children.

RIGHT
On the set of 'L'Argent de poche' (1976)
François Truffaut enjoys a moment with little Grégory. Truffaut enjoyed working with children and said that "all of a sudden they give you ten times more than you expected."

ABOVE
Still from 'L'Argent de poche' (1976)
After Sylvie (Sylvie Grézel) refuses to leave her dirty bag at home, her parents go to Sunday lunch without her. Starving, she receives food from the neighbours.

TOP LEFT
Still from 'L'Argent de poche' (1976)
Julien Leclou (Philippe Goldmann) is discovered by the janitor sleeping outside the school gates. He was thrown out of his home and spent the night on the streets.

LEFT
Still from 'L'Argent de poche' (1976)
Franck (left) and Mathieu Deluca (right) want money so they cut Richard Golfier's hair. Badly.

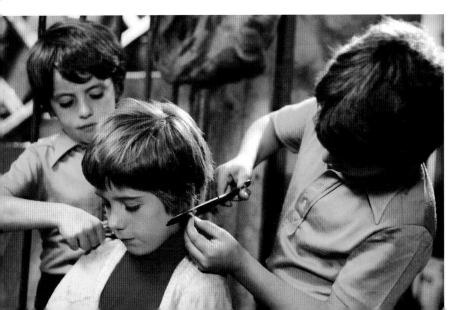

ABOVE
Still from 'L'Argent de poche' (1976)
Patrick Desmouceaux (Georges Desmouceaux) and Martine (Pascale Bruchon) meet on the train to summer camp and it becomes obvious to everybody that they like each other, so the children trick them into kissing. It was based on an incident that happened to Truffaut.

RIGHT
On the set of 'L'Argent de poche' (1976)
The two-month shoot, begun 17 July 1975, was physically exhausting because of the amount of attention that had to be given to the little actors. On 17 March 1976, the film opened to great success in Paris and went on to gross $1.5 million in America.

The desire to make a film entirely devoted to children had been in his mind since the beginning of his career. He had kept a file of incidents, press cuttings, anecdotes from the days of *Les Mistons* and *Les Quatre Cents Coups*. With the help of Suzanne Schiffman, a short scenario had been produced in 1972 and this was fleshed out in the summer of 1974. Production costs were kept to a minimum by using one location, the provincial town of Thiers. Many of the actors were citizens of the town; the rest, little known. Shooting took place mostly in a school in Thiers, in the summer holidays of 1975.

There is no story as such to *L'Argent de poche*. It is, rather, a collection of stories, a series of narratives attached to each of the multiple characters. Two youngsters emerge slowly from the group. Patrick cares for his wheelchair-bound father and is in love with Mrs Riffle, mother of his friend Laurent. Julien comes from a socially deprived background. Then there are Thomas (the newborn child of Mr and Mrs Richet) and the two-year-old Gregory (who falls from a tower block and escapes unscathed), Sylvie (who locks herself in the family flat and shouts for food), the Deluca brothers (with their scams) and Martine (who gives Patrick his first kiss). And around the children, but carefully in the background, is a range of adults: parents, teachers, a caretaker (played by the caretaker of the school in which the film was made) and the police.

Truffaut said it was his intention to portray childhood from birth to the threshold of adolescence, or as he put it in the interview he accorded the young Philippe Goldmann (Julien in the film), "Our idea really is 'from the first bottle to the first kiss.'"[72] Truffaut has spoken frequently of his motives in making the film, variously referring to "their [children's] desire for autonomy but at the same time their need for affection, something of which they are not aware"[73] and his wish to depict "children's tremendous ability to stand up to life and survive."[74] One of the most transparent reasons for the film comes in the impassioned plea on behalf of children's rights delivered by Mr Richet, the schoolteacher, at the end of the film. He refers to his own unhappy childhood, to the hard knocks of life and the need to have a tough skin. No one stands up for children. Since they cannot vote, politicians ignore them. If parents love children, that love will be returned. If they do not, the love will be directed elsewhere, since "life is such that we cannot do without loving and being loved."

Patrick's lack of a mother makes him seek love wherever he can find it. Inspired by one of Truffaut's favourite posters (travelling by train at night) and its stereotypical romantic female, he understandably falls for Mrs Riffle and in a scene repeated from *Les Quatre Cents Coups*, he encounters her in her bathrobe, legs exposed, doing her toe-nails. This image contrasts with a previous shot of her beautiful face softened romantically by the net curtain through which we see it. The archetypal dichotomy of mother as virgin and/or whore and the confusion of a young, motherless boy faced with these conflicting images are accurately and sensitively presented. For once, there is also a positive portrait of a father – and incidentally a schoolteacher – in the caring, thoughtful and articulate Mr Richet. However, there are again absent fathers: Julien's and, in a sense, Patrick's.

Somewhat atypically, the classroom is one of three locations to be presented positively. The school environment here is a far cry from that of *Les Quatre Cents Coups*. There is no rote learning here, no sarcasm, no routine humiliation of the weaker pupil. Children in Mr Richet's class participate, have a voice, are articulate and confident. In a similar vein, the unhappy home of Antoine Doinel is replaced by

"The things men do always seem puerile to me, completely childish. I see them in planes – that above all is the situation that gets me, not international flights but domestic ones. I see businessmen with ridiculous little cases and I always wonder what they are going to do. I always feel that what they are doing is trivial. Whereas the essential things in daily life, in its most day-to-day aspects: the soup to be made, the washing to be done and at the same time, the most crucial thing in life – which is continuity through children and all that – revolves around women. In the final analysis, everything outside cooking and having children doesn't really serve any great purpose."

François Truffaut [75]

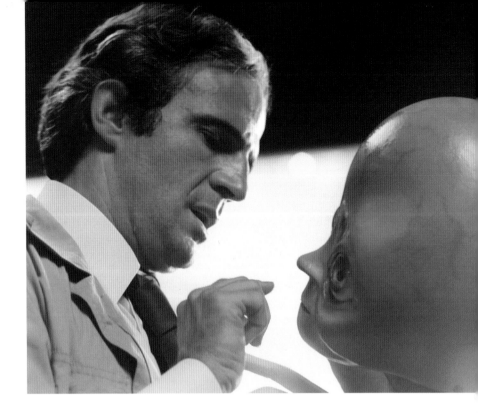

the loving environment provided for Laurent by Mr and Mrs Riffle. The third location is one that features, however fleetingly, in virtually every Truffaut film: the cinema. In *L'Argent de poche* it has a central role as a focal point for the whole community, which meets there every week, regardless of what is showing. The cinema is a haven but also a source of excitement, enchantment, escape. In this and in other respects, *L'Argent de poche* is once again in part inspired by a vision that is anachronistic. The film purportedly portrays the Thiers of 1975. In reality, much of the material within it owes more to the France of the 1940s and 1950s.

The film, released in March 1976, was an unexpected success. But Truffaut was once again exhausted and ordered to rest by his doctor. He had begun work on *L'Homme qui aimait les femmes* but was not planning to film until the autumn. His plans were disrupted by a surprise invitation from Steven Spielberg to play the part of Professor Claude Lacombe in *Close Encounters of the Third Kind*. After some hesitation he agreed, and spent time between May and early autumn filming in the USA, mostly in Mobile, Alabama. He was given an office and was able to work on *L'Homme qui aimait les femmes* in the long gaps between filming. Spielberg's big budget movies with a cast and crew of hundreds were very different from the Carrosse's modest productions, but Truffaut learned a great deal from observing and got on well with Spielberg. The experience was a positive one, he was a success in the role and was able to move on to his next project with a renewed confidence.

The Man Who Loved Women But Feared Death 1977–1984

Though not exactly the period of repose, of reading and reflection that he had envisaged, the time that elapsed between the completion of *L'Argent de poche* (early 1976) and the beginning of the shooting of *L'Homme qui aimait les femmes* was spent to good effect. Being a 'passive' actor rather than 'active' director gave him new insights. He was able to work on the new project free from the usual pressures. By the time he returned to France in September 1976, the scenario was ready and he plunged immediately into casting. Truffaut wanted to investigate further the character of Fergus that he and Charles Denner had created in *La Mariée était en noir*. Denner thus follows in the footsteps of Jean-Pierre Léaud, becoming another *alter ego* for Truffaut. Filming began on 19 October and lasted for over two months.

The film opens with the funeral of Bertrand Morane, an engineer at the Institute of Fluid Mechanics. The many mourners are exclusively female. His story is presented in flashback by Geneviève Bigey, a publisher. Relentlessly, obsessively, Bertrand seeks out women. Prompted by a rejection, he decides to write his memoirs and hires a typist. When she resigns, offended by the content, he types the rest of the manuscript himself and, on completion, sends it off to various publishers. At one of these he finds a champion, Geneviève. She visits the town where Bertrand lives to oversee the printing of the work and becomes one of his mistresses. It is Christmas. Although she makes it clear that she is free, Bertrand allows her to leave and, not wanting to be alone, pursues a woman he sees in the street and is run over by a passing car. In critical condition in his hospital bed, he awakens to the sight of a nurse's legs glanced through her tunic against the light from the corridor. He tries to get up, severing the connection with his life-support equipment and dies.

L'Homme qui aimait les femmes is a difficult film to categorise. Not for the first time, Truffaut had set out to make a comedy and while the final product is not wholly devoid of humour, it is too dark to fall into that category. The mainspring of the film can be traced to his own experience. He explained to Anne Gillain how he came to shoot the black and white sequences depicting Bertrand with his mother. One of these replicates a scene from *Les Quatre Cents Coups*, showing a young boy's conflicting emotions in the presence of a harsh and uncaring mother who flaunts her sexuality in front of him. The boy is repelled and attracted

Still from 'La Chambre verte' (1978)
Julien Davenne (François Truffaut) tries to find a permanent memorial to his wife's temporary life.

"To make a film is to improve life."
François Truffaut [76]

149

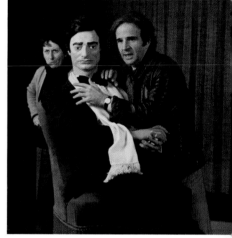

LEFT
Still from 'L'Homme qui aimait les femmes' (1977)
Some people cannot pass a bookshop without going in to browse. In the case of Bertrand Morane (Charles Denner), he is compelled to look at and talk to women. Here, as he looks at the mannequin, note how the reflection of the hand in the window seems to caress him. Not only does he need to love, but he needs to be loved in return.

ABOVE
On the set of 'L'Homme qui aimait les femmes' (1977)
François Truffaut and Suzanne Schiffman flank the dummy of Bertrand Morane, which was used in the nightmare sequence. The dummy is on display in a shop window and its suspender is rearranged by Hélène, as she previously rearranged the lingerie (see page 15). Women look at the dummy. Not only is he subject to the female gaze, but the atmosphere is like a dead body being looked at for the last time.

Still from 'L'Homme qui aimait les femmes' (1977)
While waiting at an airport, Morane imagines that all the men in suits are women with beautiful legs. Morane says: "The legs of women are the points of a compass that bestride the terrestrial globe in all directions, giving it its equilibrium and its harmony."

simultaneously and spends the rest of his life trying to win the affection and identity denied him in childhood. As Truffaut remarked 'You have with women the relationship you had with your mother.'[77]

Bertrand Morane is a serial seducer. His behaviour is compulsive. Again and again he has to prove to himself that he is capable of charming women into bed. He is a bundle of fetishes: in particular, he is obsessed with women's legs, with the swish of nylon stockings, the sway of hips in soft, loose-fitting skirts. In short, Bertrand Morane is a classic example of the male chauvinist; his focusing on part(s) of the body rather than the complete being is typical of the male gaze, which dominates most representations of woman. Truffaut was conscious of this and knew that the film would be attacked by feminists. He was not disappointed. Given his upbringing and the pre-war generation to which he belonged, it would not be surprising if Truffaut were a somewhat unreconstructed male. Bertrand's attitude to women is undeniably sexist. They are sexual objects: 'tall stems' or 'little apples,' to be placed in categories according to their sexual appeal. One loses count of the number of shots of legs, beginning in the very first frame of the film. Not only legs, but also breasts and lingerie. The case against Truffaut is irrefutable. He is, however, aware of his position and ironises it throughout.

Bertrand is not portrayed as the conventional womaniser. Truffaut makes no apology for him. He is not presented sympathetically. We see his reclusive, selfish

nature as it is. However, Bertrand is not arrogant, nor does he force his attention upon women. There is no harassment here of the kind seen in *La Peau douce*. On the contrary, he is gentle and considerate, is happy for Geneviève to drive, accepting without resentment his rejection at the hands of Hélène, owner of the lingerie shop. He is continually anxious, never elated. His behaviour is compulsive, out of control, and he is painfully unable to form a lasting relationship. While living as a couple might not offer a solution to the conundrum of relationships, neither does the lonely life of a serial seducer.

Another glimpse of Truffaut's awareness of his own chauvinism comes in the form of Bertrand's dream. As has been pointed out,[78] this dream reverses the usual roles as Bertrand finds himself in the lingerie shop window, a dummy of him being stared at by a crowd of women as Hélène adjusts his suspender. Here, the man is the object of the female gaze and, moreover, that gaze is as fetishistic as his own. Finally, we must not forget that narrative control of the film lies with a woman, Geneviève, who frames Bertrand's story within her own. Truffaut might have been a male chauvinist but he was aware of the nuances of the debate. The film was, he claimed, 'a feminist film, Truffaut style.'[79]

ABOVE
Still from 'L'Homme qui aimait les femmes' (1977)
The film revolves around stories and storytellers. Bertrand Morane is so strongly attracted to a pair of legs he saw that he smashes up his car in an effort to find them.

RIGHT
Still from 'L'Homme qui aimait les femmes' (1977)
When Morane is refused by a woman because he is too old, he decides to write his memoirs as a skirtchaser. Here he remembers Delphine Grezel (Nelly Borgeaud) who liked to make love in public places because it excited her.

LEFT
Still from 'L'Homme qui aimait les femmes' (1977)
Editor Geneviève Bigey (Brigitte Fossey) reads
the manuscript and recommends the book for
publication.

BELOW
Still from 'L'Homme qui aimait les femmes' (1977)
Bertrand Morane meets a little girl in a red
dress, Juliette (Frédérique Jamet), and talks with
her. When Morane's book is being proofed, he
changes the colour of the dress to blue, and we
see the scene again with the blue dress. In this
succinct way, Truffaut shows that often the
details of a story, and where they come from, are
just the tools he uses to tell the story.

Still from 'La Chambre verte' (1978)
Julien Davenne arranges for a life-size waxwork
figure of his dead wife to be built as a shrine to
her. The chapel was dressed with Truffaut's
personal photos of his dead friends. There are
shrines in other Truffaut films: Antoine Doinel's
shrine to Balzac burns in 'Les Quatre Cents
Coups', and Adèle has a shrine to Lieutenant
Pinson in 'L'Histoire d'Adèle H.'

Although *L'Homme qui aimait les femmes* was not yet completed, work was
already well underway on the next film, *La Chambre verte*. Truffaut's obsession
with death has been well documented. The idea for a film on the dead had
preoccupied him for several years and had been accentuated by the deaths of
numerous friends and colleagues. In an interview published in *L'Express* on 13
March 1978, he remarked, 'I have just turned 46 and already I am beginning to
be surrounded by the dead. Half of the actors who appeared in *Tirez sur le
pianiste* are gone.'[80]

   La Chambre verte, based on several short stories by Henry James, tells the story
of Julien Davenne, a survivor of the Great War, and now ten years later a writer of
obituaries for an ailing periodical, *The Globe*. He lives and works in a town in the
east of France. His sole purpose in life is to keep alive the memory of his wife Julie
who had died in 1919 at the age of 22. The eponymous 'green room' is a shrine to
her, jealously guarded by Davenne. At an auction, seeking to buy back a ring once
belonging to Julie, he meets and befriends Cécilia Mandel. The 'green room' is
damaged by fire caused by lightning. He feels he has failed to protect Julie and
commissions the making of a life-size wax model. Once he sees the model he
furiously orders it to be destroyed. Discovering by accident an old chapel damaged
during the war, he asks permission to renovate it as a shrine to his 'dear departed.'

His wish is granted and he asks Cécilia to become its guardian. She declines, not
for the first time disagreeing with Davenne over his attitude to the dead. Davenne
discovers Cécilia had been the mistress of Massigny, a man who had once been a
close friend but who had subsequently betrayed him. He becomes ill. Cécilia writes
to say that she loves him. Davenne goes to the chapel. Cécilia is there. He dies in
her arms. She lights a candle for Davenne, thus 'completing the pattern.'

Such is the overwhelming obsession with death in *La Chambre verte* and so
personal and detailed are the references, that the film is difficult of access for most
spectators. Both within the film – Davenne's discussion with the priest – and
outside it, Truffaut was at pains to make clear that *La Chambre verte* is not about a
cult of the dead, nor was it in any doctrinaire sense religious. "In *La Nuit
américaine*," he said, "there was glorification of the work of film-makers. Here [in
La Chambre verte] there is glorification of people who have counted. It's a bit like
a declaration of love, and is neither depressing, nor morbid nor sad. Rather, it's
the notion that remembering, faithfulness and fixations are stronger than the
present… We must not become detached from things and people that are no
longer talked about. Rather, if we love them, we must continue to live with them.
I refuse to forget."[81]

Most of those who have seen the film will probably find it difficult to accept the claim that it is neither morbid nor sad. Davenne's maudlin and blind obsession with his wife and his pathetic death are unlikely to have any other effect on the viewer. Like Bertrand before him, Julien seeks an absolute, this time in attempting to achieve a permanence in life rather than in death. Truffaut, like Julien, sought to keep alive the memory of those he had lost, by preserving their memory in as many ways as possible. Julien is, however, presented with a considerable degree of irony and is far from being a character without weaknesses. His desire to keep his beloved Julie alive is more like total possession than love. He is blind to the living and the feelings both of himself and those around him. This self-centredness tragically deprives him of the possibility of a new love with Cécilia. Throughout the film, she is an active force for life in stark contrast to the passive, dark and death-fixated presence of Julien. She emerges with great credit while we cannot but condemn him. To ensure our sympathy is never truly engaged, Truffaut makes Davenne commit the ultimate crime: striking the young mute child, Georges.

Once again, the pursuit of the absolute is shown to be damaging and vain. We must accept that life is provisional, even though it is painful for us to do so. Much though he would like to have kept his loved ones alive, Truffaut could no more achieve permanence in life than he could in his personal relationships. The only form of permanence man can attain is through art and above all forms of art, film, since it preserves (forever now that we have DVD?) a visual and an aural presence. Such permanence is however illusory, a good 'ruse' as Truffaut might have said, but never 'real'. He was forced to accept the stark truth that the absolute, the definitive, the permanent is beyond the grasp of man: 'But where emotions are concerned, everything seeks the permanent. A child wants his mother for life; couples in love want to love each other forever; everything in us yearns for the permanent – whereas life teaches us the provisional.'[82]

In private showings to friends, his ambitions for the film appeared to have been realised. The response was almost universally favourable. And on release on 5 April 1978, the critics concurred. The public sadly did not and *La Chambre verte* disappointed at the box office and, for once, not only in France. The failure affected Truffaut deeply because he wanted to make films that connected with the audience but he had failed to do so, even though it had been made as he had envisaged. On top of this, he had health problems and the doctor again ordered rest. This did not, however, prevent him from looking for a new scenario. As usual there were projects in hand but Truffaut was not happy with any of them. After the poor box-office performance of *La Chambre verte*, the coffers of the Carrosse again needed replenishing. What better proposition than another Doinel film?

"I'm nostalgic, totally turned towards the past. I work on my past or that of others."

François Truffaut [83]

ABOVE
Still from 'La Chambre verte' (1978)
Julien Davenne's shrine to his wife Julie is damaged by a fire.

OPPOSITE
Still from 'La Chambre verte' (1978)
Davenne refuses to forget the dead, but in doing so he fails to see that he is loved by Cécilia Mandel (Nathalie Baye). When Davenne dies, she lights a candle for him (see page 22), thus continuing the cycle.

PAGES 160/161
Still from 'L'Amour en fuite' (1979)
Truffaut wrote that Antoine Doinel (Jean-Pierre Léaud) is 'always on the run, always late, a young man in a rush... Antoine should stop... running away... he should take advantage of the present... should stop settling a score with his mother through every girl he meets.'

Still from 'L'Amour en fuite' (1979)
Antoine finds his new love Sabine (Dorothée, in photo) using the detective skills he acquired in 'Baisers volés.' When a man breaks up with a girl over the phone and tears up her photo, Antoine pieces the photo together, falls in love with the girl in the photo and then woos her without telling her about the photo.

"The immense sadness of films without women. I hate war films, except for the moment when the soldier takes out of his pocket the photo of a woman."

François Truffaut 84

Truffaut was hesitant. He had not intended to return to Doinel after *Domicile conjugal*. Could the character retain its charm in adulthood? With a small budget, provided for the first time by the Carrosse alone, Truffaut decided to go ahead. Filming began at the end of May 1978 and took just 28 days. The editing, in contrast, took four months.

Antoine, now a proofreader, has spent the night with new partner Sabine. It is the day of his divorce. After he emerges from the court building, he is recognised, at a distance, by Colette, now a lawyer. Having earlier promised to go to a party with Sabine, he phones to tell her he cannot go, as he must take his son Alphonse to the station. There he sees Colette, who is about to leave on another train. She is holding a copy of his autobiography, *Les Salades de l'amour* (*Love's Confusions*). He leaps on the train. At first, she is delighted to see him. Antoine recounts the plot of the novel he is writing: a young man finds the torn-up photo of a girl and painstakingly puts it together again, falling in love with her. After strenuous efforts he locates her. They get together but later drift apart. In Colette's couchette, Antoine makes a pass at her. She pretends to be a high-class prostitute. He pulls the emergency cord and flees. Sabine meanwhile has decided to end their relationship because Antoine is unwilling to make a commitment. When he finally catches up with her, she throws his letters at him in disgust. Mr Lucien, former lover of Antoine's mother, meets Antoine by chance. They lunch together and visit the cemetery where Antoine's mother is buried. Colette meets Christine; they laugh at

Still from 'L'Amour en fuite' (1979)
At the end of the film Antoine tells Sabine how he found her. He has not told her before because, "All my life I've hidden my feelings, never saying anything directly." They agree to stay together, not knowing if their love will last, but pretending it will.

LEFT
Still from 'L'Amour en fuite' (1979)
Antoine's first love Colette (Marie-France Pisier) reads his autobiography 'Les Salades de l'amour' and laughs at the discrepancies between what really happened (seen as flashbacks from 'Antoine et Colette') and what he writes. This highlights the fact that there are differences between what really happened in Truffaut's life and how he portrayed it in his films.

belonging to the Club of Antoine Doinel's Ex's. They compare notes and recall Antoine's infidelity with Liliane. Antoine finally manages to get Sabine to listen to him. He tells her the true story of how he had come to meet her: he had found her torn-up photo, fallen in love and tracked her down. She is won back and the film ends with their agreeing to live together 'as if' it would be forever.

Truffaut was as reluctant and hesitant regarding *L'Amour en fuite* as Antoine is in his relationship with Sabine. If Truffaut did not like it, his public did and the film provided the success he craved and the funds the Carrosse needed. What he saw as a money-spinner done on the cheap nevertheless contains new insights and new perspectives on ongoing themes. Antoine is inevitably at the heart of the film, whether on screen or off: 'He is a kind of marginal figure though he is not aware of it himself... He can't tell others what to do, he is no good at sport. There are only limitations with Antoine and very few positives... He is the opposite of an exceptional character, the opposite of a hero, but what makes him different from ordinary people is that we never see him in a normal state of mind. He is either profoundly disappointed, full of despair... or else he is elated and fired with great enthusiasm.'[85] Responsibilities of parenthood, the trauma of divorce, the harsh reality of making a living appear to have made no impact. He has learned little and as always dashes hither and thither to little purpose or effect. And yet it is his defects that protect him from the world and constitute his appeal. Léaud is as persuasive as ever and the character is possibly now closer to him than it is to its creator.

One of the most telling episodes in the film is the meeting with Mr Lucien, which allows us to see another side of Antoine's mother. Unlikely though Mr Lucien's opinion of her might seem to us – he presents her as 'a little bird' and 'an anarchist' – she is portrayed as having loved her son. The scene closes with a lingering superimposition of her face over her grave accompanied by Delerue's lyrical score. We cannot but be moved by this belated tribute to and recognition of Truffaut's mother.

So dissatisfied was Truffaut with *L'Amour en fuite* that he labelled it 'a swindle.'[86] His (by now customary) low spirits following completion of a project were exacerbated by a number of possible new projects all of which for one reason or another failed to come to fruition. Finally, at the end of April 1979, he brought together two of his files: one a possible film on theatre, the other on the period of the Occupation. He and Suzanne Schiffman worked together to fuse the two projects. They read extensively – memoirs of actors and directors, newspapers, histories – and added to these their own recollections and those of colleagues and friends. The scenario was enhanced by Jean-Claude Grumberg, a playwright and scriptwriter, who made an important contribution, particularly regarding the role of Lucas Steiner. It also fulfilled Truffaut's desire to cast Gérard Depardieu and Catherine Deneuve in the same film.

Le Dernier Métro opens shortly before the Germans occupied the 'free zone' in 1942 and ends with the Liberation. Bernard Granger arrives at the Théâtre Montmartre to audition for a part in a new play, *La Disparue* (*The Woman who Disappeared*). The theatre is managed by the actress Marion Steiner, wife of the theatre's director, Lucas Steiner, a Jew who is said to have fled to South America. One by one we meet those who work at the theatre, including Nadine Marsac, an aspiring young actress, Jean-Loup Cottins, the actor and director replacing Lucas, Arlette, who is responsible for costumes and Raymond, the stage manager. Later

OPPOSITE TOP
On the set of 'L'Amour en fuite' (1979)
Truffaut directs with Nestor Almendros behind the camera and Florent Bazin, the son of Janine and André Bazin, as an assistant cameraman.

OPPOSITE BOTTOM
On the set of 'L'Amour en fuite' (1979)
At the train station, Antoine Doinel sees Colette on a departing train, so they miss each other. Here Jean-Pierre Léaud and François Truffaut discuss how Antoine would shrug his shoulders. The shot is edited out and only Colette shrugs.

Still from 'Le Dernier Métro' (1980)
In occupied Paris during World War Two, the great actress Marion Steiner (Catherine Deneuve) must look after her husband's theatre because he has disappeared. In fact, Lucas Steiner (Heinz Bennent) is hiding in the basement of the theatre, giving acting notes to his wife and listening to the perfomances. In this scene they are reading 'Les Décombres' by Lucien Rebatet.

we meet Daxiat, drama critic from the *Je suis partout*, a newspaper supportive of collaboration. Rehearsals for *La Disparue*, a Norwegian play translated into French, begin. We learn that Lucas Steiner is in fact in hiding in the theatre cellar where Marion visits him regularly. Only she knows he is there. The play has its first night and is a success. Bernard has been liaising with a friend, Christian, who is a member of the Resistance. He informs Marion that he is to leave the theatre to join the Resistance. She slaps him angrily across the face, partly in disillusionment at his putting theatre second to something else but also because she is in love with him. On his last night they make love. The Allies reach Paris. Lucas emerges from his cellar. Daxiat flees. In the final sequence, Marion visits a wounded and dispirited Bernard in hospital. It transpires that this is the final scene of a play. Lucas Steiner comes on stage to acknowledge the applause. Standing between them, Marion takes each one by the hand.

The film was Truffaut's most successful in terms of box-office receipts both in France and abroad. It was seen by more than a million people in Paris alone. It was not, however, without its critics, whose main charge was that the film, portraying one of the most harrowing episodes in France's history, is optimistic and naïve, nostalgic and charming. They also claimed that it focuses primarily on relationships at the expense of a realistic portrayal of occupied France. Anne Gillain put this point to Truffaut. His response brings us back to a number of his key concerns. While accepting that the film was less critical than it could have been, he claims that it does portray the "day-to-day cruelties." Typically, he defends the majority of French people who neither joined the Resistance nor collaborated, "My film is indulgent towards those who did not take sides, towards those who continued to do their job as if nothing had changed... I do not judge France, I believe that, quite simply, it waited."[88] He explained that whereas usually his characters had

Still from 'Le Dernier Métro' (1980)
Bernard Granger (Gérard Depardieu) is hired to act opposite Marion Steiner in 'La Disparue' (The Woman who Disappeared). He is in love with Marion but she remains icy towards him in real life. On stage, however, she is obviously in love. Is she only acting in real life?

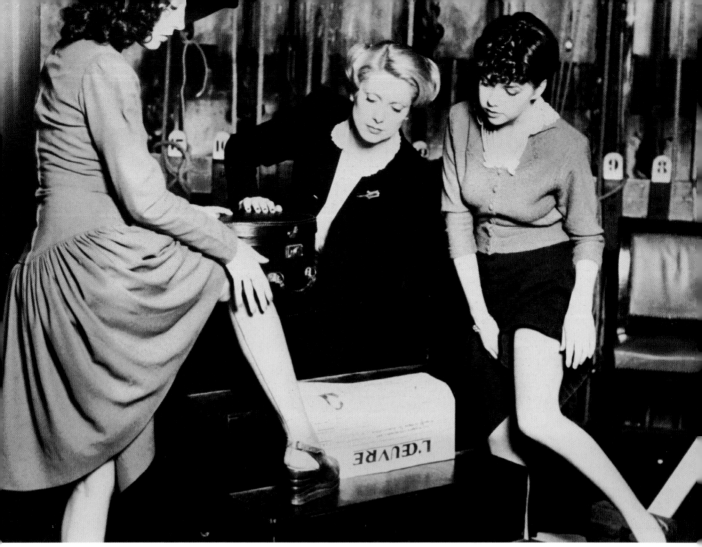

ABOVE
Still from 'Le Dernier Métro' (1980)
Martine (Martine Simonet), Marion Steiner and
Nadine Marsac (Sabine Haudepin) discuss how
to stay feminine during wartime. Since silk
stockings are so rare, they shave their legs and
cover them in make-up. The film is full of
information about how people lived during the
Occupation.

RIGHT
Still from 'Le Dernier Métro' (1980)
Bernard Granger, substitute director Jean-Loup
Cottins (Jean Poiret), Marion Steiner and Nadine
Marsac rehearse the play. Lucas can hear
everything because their voices carry through
the pipes down to the basement.

obsessions, which they pursued inexorably, most of the characters in this film were forced to compromise. Truffaut is restating, in a different way and in a different context, his preoccupation with the definitive and the provisional.[89] In this film those who took sides, whether by joining the Resistance (Christian and, ultimately, Bernard) or by collaborating (Daxiat), represent the 'definitive.' Marion and most of those working with her make compromises on a daily basis in order to survive and to preserve the supremacy of what they believe in: the theatre.

At the heart of the film is the Marion-Lucas-Bernard triangle. Having suppressed her feelings for most of the film, Marion's passion for Bernard erupts in the final sequences. She had, however, strongly denied Bernard's charge that she no longer loved her husband and for a moment we are left in doubt. The concluding sequence gives yet another statement on love: on this occasion, the solution is a 'ménage à trois.' By now, it is clear that there is no single solution to the conundrum of love. A positive feature of *Le Dernier Métro* is the presence of two homosexual relationships: both Jean-Loup and Arlette are presented sympathetically. Or to put it more pertinently, they are presented in the same way as their colleagues, there is no distinction on the basis of sexual orientation.

Although the harsh realities of deportation, betrayal and torture are omitted, *Le Dernier Métro* does give an authentic picture of Paris during the Occupation: the shots in the metro (borrowed from Franju's 1958 film, *La Première nuit*[90]), the ubiquitous presence of the Germans and their uniforms, the clandestine activities of the Resistance, the growing of tobacco in a tiny plot, a mother washing a boy's hair because a German had ruffled it, the ruses women employed to disguise the absence of nylons, the songs, the newspapers and the language. Truffaut's famous penchant for 'ruse' and ingenuity probably stemmed from his own childhood and the need to 'make do,' particularly in the war years and immediately after. The rich inventiveness of the characters here mirrors Truffaut's delight in finding ways of circumventing problems: no tobacco – grow your own; forced to wear the Jewish star – cover it up with your scarf; power cuts – rig up headlamps and power them with two bicycles. This mass of detail was the product of the careful research

"I am attracted to characters whom society marginalises, emotionally and morally."

François Truffaut [91]

Still from 'Le Dernier Métro' (1980)
Marion Steiner tries to save the theatre from closing by appealing to the Germans.

TOP
On the set of 'Le Dernier Métro' (1980)
Truffaut shows Depardieu how to attack Jean-Louis Richard.

ABOVE
Still from 'Le Dernier Métro' (1980)
Bernard Granger attacks Daxiat (Jean-Louis Richard). Daxiat is a theatre critic for the anti-Semitic newspaper 'Je suis partout' and Bernard demands that he apologise for his outrageous review. Marion then reprimands Bernard because only Daxiat can gain the consent of the censors, so Daxiat could close the theatre. This incident was based on Jean Marais' attack on anti-Semitic critic Alain Laubreaux, who had insulted Jean Cocteau in 1941.

LEFT
On the set of 'Le Dernier Métro' (1980)
Truffaut frames the audience.

Still from 'La Femme d'à côté' (1981)
Mathilde Bauchard (Fanny Ardant) is the femme
fatale who will ruin Bernard Coudray's life

Truffaut and Suzanne Schiffman had undertaken. Its humour and concentration on the minutiae of daily life contributed to the impression that this was a nostalgic and biased account of the period.

As he began shooting *Le Dernier Métro*, Truffaut was already planning his next project. As with *L'Histoire d'Adèle H.*, it was again, in part at least, inspired by a 'coup de foudre.' Where earlier it had been Isabelle Adjani whom he had seen on the stage, here it was Fanny Ardant, whom he first saw on French TV. The main themes of *La Femme d'à côté* have their origins in his relationship with Catherine Deneuve; as early as 1972 he had written a short scenario based on their affair. In 1980 he worked with Jean Aurel on a new scenario and at a later point Suzanne Schiffman made an important contribution. The final version came together very quickly in early 1981. Locations were found near Grenoble and shooting took place in spring 1981.

Bernard and Arlette Coudray live in a small village in the country with their young son, Thomas. Philippe and Mathilde Bauchard, recently married, move in opposite. Bernard and Mathilde had a tumultuous affair eight years previously. Their affair resumes. Bernard becomes jealous and assaults Mathilde at a party at the Bauchards' house. Mathilde has a breakdown. The Bauchards leave. A short time later, Bernard awakes one night and, investigating a banging door in the empty Bauchard house, finds Mathilde. They make love. Mathilde has a gun and shoots Bernard before killing herself.

After *L'Histoire d'Adèle H.*, *La Femme d'à côté* is another study of *amour fou*, of an obsessive and destructive passion, which on this occasion is shared by the two protagonists. The first period of their turbulent and highly charged relationship had been ended, eight years previously, when Bernard left Mathilde, who then suffered a nervous breakdown. After a brief, failed marriage to another man, she got married a second time, to the gentle and considerate Philippe. Bernard had married Arlette and led a calm, largely uneventful life. Without perhaps being wholly conscious of

"I immediately spotted and appreciated in Fanny Ardant the qualities I most frequently look for in the protagonists of my films: vitality, courage, enthusiasm, humour, intensity but also, to counterbalance these, a taste for secrecy, a wild side, a touch of savagery and above all something vibrant."

François Truffaut [93]

Still from 'La Femme d'à côté' (1981)
The disturbing painting comes to life. In a
jealous rage, Bernard attacks Mathilde at a
party.

Femme d'à côté. We were looking at a night scene in which Fanny Ardant was
walking around the house in a raincoat. Someone said, "It reminds me of a thriller."
And Fanny Ardant did indeed have the look of a heroine from a thriller."[96]

   Vivement dimanche! has much in common with *Tirez sur le pianiste*. Both are
based on adaptations of American novels, both subvert genre, are shot in black and
white, and have a strong vein of comedy. The novel chosen to provide source
material was Charles Williams' *The Long Saturday Night* and Truffaut worked again
with Suzanne Schiffman and Jean Aurel. They were broadly faithful to the opening
and concluding sections of the original but made major structural changes to the
remainder. Truffaut wanted to ensure that the focal point of the action was the
female (and not the male) lead. Truffaut's gradual move towards studio-based
filming is confirmed here by the use of a large disused clinic near Hyères in which
numerous sets were built and where most of the film was shot.

   The film opens with the murder of Massoulier on a hunting trip. Julien Vercel,
an estate agent, was also out shooting that morning. His relationship with his wife
Marie-Christine is in difficulties, largely due to her absences and strange behaviour.
She returns from one of her trips and she and Julien have a row. Julien is invited to
the police station in connection with the murder and returns home to discover the
body of his wife. He realises that he is compromised and retreats to his agency.

are magic." Julien and Barbara marry.

Vivement dimanche! functions on several levels. It is genuinely a 'whodunnit' in that suspense over who has committed the crimes is sustained until the penultimate sequence. It is a thriller, although an unconventional example of the genre. At the same time, it is a Hollywood-style romantic comedy. On a fourth level are the more serious concerns of its director: concerns now familiar to us even if they are always presented from a fresh perspective. Just as with *Tirez sur le pianiste*, Truffaut adheres closely to the iconography of the *film noir*. Much of the film is shot at night, and in the rain. The heroine wears the obligatory trenchcoat. There are nightclubs, prostitutes and a splendid femme fatale in Marie-Christine. There are guns, murders and a revolving wall that provides a vital clue. And of course, numerous red herrings to keep us guessing. Crucially, it is shot in black and white, a brave decision in 1982 when colour had become virtually obligatory. But it is always evident that Truffaut is subverting the genre rather than making a genre film. As with *Tirez sur le pianiste*, the film does not restrict itself to one genre and borrows from romantic comedy. A central source of interest is the tempestuous relationship of the leading characters. In the best Hollywood tradition, they begin with arguments and disagreements, even physical attacks, but end up inevitably in each other's arms.

But the subversion takes place on other, deeper levels. This is, as Truffaut pointed out, a film without gangsters or detectives, where the investigation is led by a normal person.[98] Moreover this normal person, a secretary, is a woman. The usually taut plot of the thriller is disrupted by the insertion of 'gratuitous' episodes such as the sequences dealing with the rehearsal for the play in which Barbara also plays the lead. Similarly, the action is derailed in key scenes by diversions such as the Albanian seeking political asylum, or the business with the tap involving Police Superintendent Santelli. And finally, just in case we have been taken in by the apparatus of the thriller genre, the plot of the whole film is unstitched in Maître Clément's final words, 'Everything I did, I did for women. I love to look at them, to touch them, to smell them, to enjoy them and give them pleasure. Women are magic, so I became a magician.' We have come full circle. What purported to be a thriller, was really an investigation of another of Truffaut's obsessives in search of

ABOVE
Still from 'Vivement dimanche!' (1983)
Marie-Christine Vercel (Caroline Sihol) tries to seduce her husband Julien (Jean-Louis Trintignant) after admitting to him that she has committed adultery.

OPPOSITE TOP
Still from 'Vivement dimanche!' (1983)
Julien Vercel fired his secretary Barbara Becker (Fanny Ardant), but she helps him after he is suspected of murdering his wife and her lover. But the pair still argue like a married couple. Barbara says: "It's really unfair. If a boss can fire me why can't I fire him?"

OPPOSITE BOTTOM
Still from 'Vivement dimanche!' (1983)
The murderer is surrounded. "Women are magic," he explains. "Everything I did, I did for women."

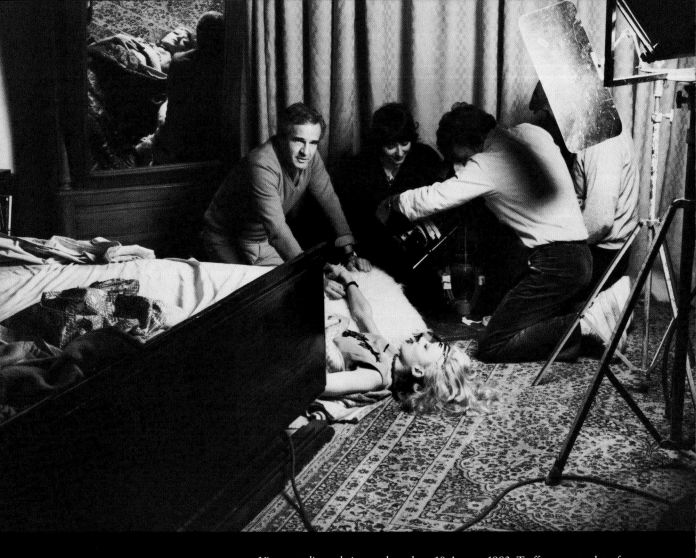

On the set of 'Vivement dimanche!' (1983)
Truffaut kneels over Caroline Sihol, who plays the murdered Marie-Christine Vercel. Notice the duvet and blanket keeping Sihol warm while the camera moves along her body to the watch on her wrist.

Vivement dimanche! was released on 10 August 1983. Truffaut spent a lot of time promoting the film, whilst simultaneously developing a synopsis of *La Petite Voleuse* (filmed by Claude Miller in 1988), updating his seminal book on Hitchcock and talking with Gérard Depardieu about various projects. On an August evening, at the house he was renting in Normandy and following an afternoon's work with Claude de Givray, Truffaut experienced what de Givray described as 'a fire-cracker going off in his head.'[99] Doctors found a brain tumour and the operation went well. At the end of September, Fanny Ardant gave birth to a daughter, Joséphine, Truffaut's third daughter. For the next year Truffaut continued to work on possible scenarios and began work on an autobiography. However, his condition deteriorated in late September and he was re-admitted to hospital where he died on 21 October 1984. His funeral three days later, though attended by thousands, had one feature in common with that of Bertrand Morane.

ABOVE
On the set of 'Vivement dimanche!' (1983)
When Barbara Becker dresses as a prostitute to infiltrate the Red Angel club run by Louison (Jean-Louis Richard, back to us), she looks through a bathroom window to spy on Louison (see page 23). This is her point of view shot being filmed. Truffaut is in the window and Suzanne Schiffman is on the left.

PAGES 182/183
On the set of 'Vivement dimanche!' (1983)
François Truffaut (right) discusses a scene with Fanny Ardant and Jean-Louis Trintignant on the

Chronology

ABOVE
Family photo
François on vacation with his stepfather Roland Truffaut.

RIGHT
Auberge de la Colombe d'Or, Saint-Paul-de-Vence (July 1962)
François Truffaut with Madeleine and Laura.

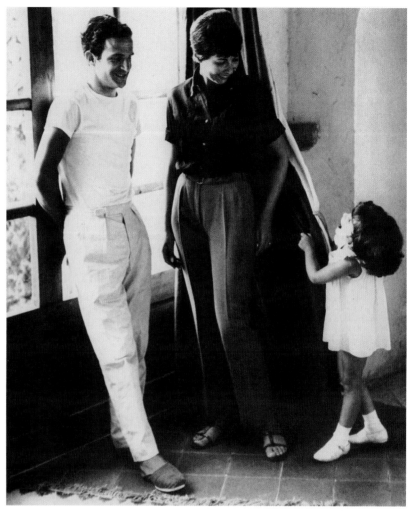

1932 Born 6 February to Janine de Monferrand in Paris.

1933 Janine marries Roland Truffaut, an architect, on 9 November. Roland accepts her child, born to an 'unknown father' although, for the first ten years of his life, François is mostly cared for by firstly a wet-nurse and then his maternal grandmother.

1942 Grandmother dies, moves in with his mother and stepfather.

1938–45 Pursues a chequered educational career in a variety of schools. By the age of 12 he is already a regular cinema-goer. On leaving formal education (and home), tries his hand at various jobs and begins attending film clubs. His attempt, in 1947, to set up his own club with his close friend Robert Lachenay is a financial disaster.

1948 For Roland Truffaut, the debts incurred by this failed enterprise are the last straw. He turns his adopted son over to the police and François subsequently spends time in a juvenile remand home at Villejuif. André Bazin and his wife, Janine, provide shelter and work opportunities.

1950 His first published articles appear in *Elle* and other newspapers and reviews. In October, suddenly decides to

undertake his military service and by the end of the year is posted in Germany. Quickly regrets his decision and deserts in July 1951. After spells in prison and hospital he is discharged. Bazin again comes to the rescue.

1953 With the support of Bazin, begins writing for *Cahiers du cinéma*. In January 1954, his now famous article 'Une certaine tendance du cinéma français' appears in the *Cahiers*. In it, he attacks the old guard and suggests French cinema take a new direction.

1954 Makes his first film, an eight-minute short entitled *Une visite*. The film is never released commercially.

1955–56 Intermittently works as assistant to the Italian director Roberto Rossellini. None of the projects on which he works come to fruition but the collaboration is richly rewarding.

1956 At the Venice Film Festival in September, meets Madeleine Morgenstern, daughter of a well-known film distributor-producer. They marry on 29 October 1957 and have two daughters, Laura and Eva. Though they later divorce, they maintain a close relationship until his death.

1957 Shoots *Les Mistons* (23 minutes) in the summer in

Nîmes, largely with funds provided by Madeleine's father, though he was not aware of this arrangement at the time. To manage the operation, Truffaut sets up Les Films du Carrosse. From these small beginnings grows the company which will help him retain his independent stance throughout his career. *Les Mistons* is shown out of competition at the Tours Short-Film Festival in November and at the Brussels Festival of World Cinema in February 1958 where it wins the award for Best Director.

1959 The success of *Les Mistons* encourages him to turn his back on film criticism and take up directing full time. He plunges himself in to the making of *Les Quatre Cents Coups* which is chosen as an official French selection for the Cannes Film Festival. It takes the Festival by storm, winning the Grand Prix. The New Wave is born. Jean-Pierre Léaud and his alter ego Antoine Doinel become household names overnight.

1960 Visits the USA to receive the New York critics prize for Best Foreign Film (for *Les Quatre Cents Coups*) and meets Helen Scott who will later serve as interpreter-translator for a seminal book of interviews with Alfred Hitchcock. The financial success of *Les Quatre Cents Coups* enables him to experiment. His second full-length film, *Tirez sur le pianiste*, starring Charles Aznavour, is released on 25 November to mixed reviews.

1962–66 Now firmly established as one of the young Turks of French cinema, makes four films in five years beginning with the celebrated *Jules et Jim* and ending with the less successful *Fahrenheit 451*, shot in the UK in 1966 and starring Julie Christie. In between come the second Doinel film, the 29-minute short *Antoine et Colette* which is his contribution to the compilation film *L'Amour à vingt ans* (1962), and *La Peau douce* (1964).

1967 The product of five years' work, *Hitchcock by Truffaut* was published in November 1967. Based on a series of interviews with Hitchcock, the book was an immediate success and fulfilled his long-held desire to publish a book of his own.

1968 *La Mariée était en noir*, starring Jeanne Moreau is well received by critics and public alike. He is already at work on *Baisers volés*, the third film in the Doinel cycle, first shown at the Avignon Festival in August 1968 and another outright success. Behind the scenes, life moves into turbulent mode as he enters public life protesting against the

sacking of Henri Langlois, director of the Cinémathèque before in May participating in the closing down of the Cannes Festival. At the same time he discovers his father is Roland Lévy, a Jew.

1969–72 Another fertile period in which he makes four films: *La Sirène du Mississippi* (1969), *L'Enfant sauvage* (1969), the fourth Doinel film *Domicile conjugal* (1970), *Les Deux Anglaises et le Continent* (1971) and *Une belle fille comme moi* (1972). A relationship with Catherine Deneuve begun during the shooting of *La Sirène du Mississippi* ends in December 1970 provoking a lengthy and deep depression.

1973 *Day for Night* (*La Nuit américaine*) is a major hit and wins the Oscar for Best Foreign Film.

1975 Publication of second book, *Les Films de ma vie*.

1975–77 Energy restored, makes three more films in rapid succession: *L'Histoire d'Adèle H.* (1975), *L'Argent de poche* (1976) and *L'Homme qui aimait les femmes* (1977). Appears as Claude Lacombe in Spielberg's *Close Encounters of the Third Kind*.

1978 *La Chambre verte*, which is not well received, is released in April.

1979 *L'Amour en fuite* premieres in January, bringing the Doinel films to a successful conclusion.

1980 *Le Dernier Métro* starring Deneuve and Depardieu is an outstanding commercial and critical success and wins ten Césars (French equivalent of the Oscars).

1981 Depardieu is retained for *La Femme d'à côté* co-starring with Fanny Ardant.

1983 *Vivement dimanche!* is well received on release in August. In September, Fanny Ardant, having become Truffaut's partner, gives birth to his third daughter, Joséphine. Just prior to her birth, Truffaut is taken ill.

1984 Truffaut dies on 21 October in the American hospital at Neuilly, aged 52.

ABOVE
Robert Lachenay at rue François Truffaut

BOTTOM LEFT
Alfred Hitchcock and François Truffaut
Truffaut first met Hitchcock on the set of 'To Catch a Thief' in 1954.

BELOW
On the set of 'Le Déjeuner sur l'herbe' (1959)
Truffaut visited Jean Renoir on the set of 'French Cancan' in 1954 and they became close friends.

Filmography

Une visite *(1954)*
Crew: *Director/Script* François Truffaut,
Producer & Assistant Director Robert Lachenay,
Camera Jacques Rivette, *Editor* Alain Resnais,
B&W, 7 minutes 40 seconds.
Cast: Francis Cognany, Florence Doniol-Valcroze,
Laura Mauri, Jean-José Richer.
Une visite is a short film about a young single
mother who takes in a lodger.

Les Mistons
(UK/USA: The Mischief Makers, 1957)
Crew: *Director/Script* François Truffaut,
Producer Robert Lachenay, *Assistant Directors*
Claude de Givray & Alain Jeannel, *Short Story*
'Les Mistons' in *Les Virginales* Maurice Pons,
Music Maurice Le Roux, *Camera* Jean Malige,
Editor Cécile Decugis, B&W, 23 minutes.
Cast: Gérard Blain (Gérard), Bernadette Lafont
(Bernadette).
Les Mistons is a short film about a group of boys
who follow and torment two young lovers, one
summer in Provence.

Une histoire d'eau *(1958)*
Crew: *Director* François Truffaut, *Producer* Pierre
Braunberger, *Production Manager* Roger
Fleytoux, *Script & Editor* Jean-Luc Godard,
Camera Michel Latouche, *Sound* Jacques
Maumont, B&W, 18 minutes.
Cast: Jean-Claude Brialy (The Man), Caroline Dim
(The Girl).
Une histoire d'eau was begun by François Truffaut
and completed by Jean-Luc Godard. It was filmed
on the outskirts of Paris during floods.

Les Quatre Cents Coups
(UK/USA: The 400 Blows, 1959)
Crew: *Director/Script* François Truffaut,
Executive Producer Georges Charlot, *Assistant
Directors* Philippe de Broca with Alain Jeannel,
Francis Cognany, Robert Bober, *Camera* Henri
Decaë with Jean Rabier, Michèle de Possel, *Sound*
Jean-Claude Marchetti with Jean Labussière,
Music Jean Constantin, *Editor* Marie-Joseph
Yoyotte with Cécile Decugis, B&W, 93 minutes.
Cast: Jean-Pierre Léaud (Antoine Doinel), Claire
Maurier (Mother), Albert Rémy (Stepfather),
Patrick Auffay (René), Guy Decomble (Teacher),
Jeanne Moreau (Woman in street).

Les Quatre Cents Coups describes the life and
(mis-)adventures of a young boy, Antoine Doinel,
living in a cramped apartment in Paris with his
mother and stepfather.

Tirez sur le pianiste
*(UK: Shoot the Pianist, USA: Shoot the Piano
Player, 1960)*
Crew: *Director* François Truffaut, *Producer* Pierre
Braunberger, *Production Managers* Serge Komor
& Roger Fleytoux, *Assistant Directors* Francis
Cognany & Robert Bober, *Novel Down There*
David Goodis, *Script* François Truffaut & Jean
Gruault, *Camera*: Raoul Coutard, *Editor*

Claudine Bouché, *Continuity* Suzanne Schiffman, *Sound* Jacques Gallois, *Music* Georges Delerue, *Art Direction* Jacques Mély, B&W, 85 minutes.
Cast: Charles Aznavour (Charlie Koller), Marie Dubois (Léna), Nicole Berger (Thérésa), Michèle Mercier (Clarisse), Albert Rémy (Chico), Serge Davri (Plyne), Richard Kanayan (Fido).
Tirez sur le pianiste is an off-beat thriller about a shy former concert pianist, now working in a bar in Paris, finding and losing love.

Jules et Jim (UK/USA: *Jules and Jim*, 1962)
Crew: *Director* François Truffaut, *Executive Producer* Marcel Berbert, *Assistant Directors* Georges Pellegrin & Robert Bober, *Novel* Pierre-Henri Roché, *Script* François Truffaut & Jean Gruault, *Camera* Raoul Coutard, *Music* Georges Delerue, *Editor* Claudine Bouché, B&W, 100 minutes.
Cast: Jeanne Moreau (Catherine), Oskar Werner (Jules), Henri Serre (Jim), Boris Bassiak (Albert), Vanna Urbino (Gilberte), Sabine Haudepin (Sabine).
Jules et Jim is the story of two men who love the same woman and is set in Paris and Germany before, during and after the Great War.

Antoine et Colette (1962)
Episode in the compilation film *L'Amour à vingt ans* (*Love at Twenty*, 1962)
Crew: *Director/Script* François Truffaut, *Executive Producer* Philippe Dussart, *Production Manager* Pierre Roustang, *Assistant Director* Georges Pellegrin, *Camera* Raoul Coutard, *Editor* Claudine Bouché, *Continuity* Suzanne Schiffman, *Music* Georges Delerue, *Photographer* Henri

Cartier-Bresson, *Artistic Advisor* Jean de Baroncelli, B&W, 29 minutes.
Cast: Jean-Pierre Léaud (Antoine Doinel), Marie-France Pisier (Colette), Patrick Auffay (René).
Antoine et Colette continues the story of Antoine Doinel, now an adolescent and in love with Colette.

La Peau douce
(UK: *Silken Skin*, USA *The Soft Skin*, 1964)
Crew: *Director* François Truffaut, *Executive Producer* Marcel Berbert, *Production Manager* Georges Charlot, *Assistant Director* Jean-François Adam, *Script* François Truffaut & Jean-Louis Richard, *Camera* Raoul Coutard, *Editor* Claudine Bouché, *Continuity* Suzanne Schiffman, *Music* Georges Delerue, B&W, 115 minutes.
Cast: Françoise Dorléac (Nicole), Jean Desailly (Pierre Lachenay), Nelly Benedetti (Franca Lachenay), Sabine Haudepin (Sabine Lachenay).
*La Peau douce i*s a melodrama about adultery and murder, based on a true story.

Fahrenheit 451 (1966)
Crew: *Director* François Truffaut, *Producer* Lewis M. Allen, *Associate Producer* Micky Delamar, *Assistant Director* Bryan Coates, *Novel* Ray Bradbury, *Script* François Truffaut, Jean-Louis Richard, David Rudkin, Helen Scott, *Camera* Nicholas Roeg, *Editor* Thom Noble, *Continuity* Kay Manders, *Music* Bernard Herrmann, *Sound* Bib McPhee, *Art Direction/Costumes* Syd Cain & Tony Walton, Colour, 113 minutes.
Cast: Oskar Werner (Montag), Julie Christie (Lynda and Clarisse), Cyril Cusack (The Captain), Anton Diffring (Fabian).
Fahrenheit 451 is a science-fiction film about a

totalitarian regime where books are considered dangerous and firemen are sent to burn them.

La Mariée était en noir
(UK/USA: *The Bride Wore Black*, 1967)
Crew: *Director* François Truffaut, *Executive Producer* Marcel Berbert, *Production Manager* Georges Charlot, *Assistant Director* Jean Chayrou and Roland Thénot, *Novel The Bride Wore Black* William Irish, *Script* François Truffaut & Jean-Louis Richard, *Camera* Raoul Coutard, *Editor* Claudine Bouché with Yann Dedet, *Continuity* Suzanne Schiffman, *Sound* René Levert, *Music* Bernard Herrmann, *Art Direction* Pierre Guffroy, Colour, 107 minutes.

Cast: Jeanne Moreau (Julie Kohler), Claude Rich (Bliss), Jean-Claude Brialy (Corey), Michel Bouquet (Coral), Michael Lonsdale (Morane), Charles Denner (Fergus), Daniel Boulanger (Delvaux).
La Mariée était en noir is a psychological thriller about revenge.

Baisers volés *(UK/USA: Stolen Kisses, 1968)*
Crew: *Director* François Truffaut, *Executive Producer* Marcel Berbert, *Production Manager* Roland Thénot, *Assistant Director* Jean-José Richer, *Script* François Truffaut with Claude de Givray & Bernard Revon, *Camera* Denys Clerval, *Music* Antoine Duhamel, *Continuity* Suzanne Schiffman, *Editor* Agnès Guillemot, *Sound* René Levert, *Art Direction* Claude Pignot, Colour, 90 minutes.
Cast: Jean-Pierre Léaud (Antoine Doinel), Claude Jade (Christine), Delphine Seyrig (Mme Tabard), Harry-Max (M Henri), Michel Lonsdale (M Tabard).
Baisers volés is the third film in the Doinel cycle. It

is a light-hearted comedy about the life and loves of Antoine.

La Sirène du Mississippi
(USA: Mississippi Mermaid, 1969)
Crew: *Director/Script* François Truffaut, *Executive Producer* Marcel Berbert, *Production Managers* Claude Miller & Roland Thénot, *Assistant Director* Jean-José Richer, *Novel Waltz into Darkness* William Irish, *Camera* Denys Clerval, *Editor* Agnès Guillemot with Yann Dedet, *Continuity* Suzanne Schiffman, *Sound* René Levert, *Music* Antoine Duhamel, *Art Direction* Claude Pignot with Jean-Pierre Kohut-Svelko, Colour, 120 minutes.
Cast: Jean-Paul Belmondo (Louis Mahé), Catherine Deneuve (Marion/Julie Roussel), Marcel Berbert (Jardine), Michel Bouquet (Comolli).
La Sirène du Mississippi, set mainly in Reunion and in the South of France, is a Hitchcock-style psychological thriller about love and deception.

L'Enfant sauvage
(UK/USA: The Wild Child, 1969)
Crew: *Director* François Truffaut, *Executive Producer* Marcel Berbert, *Production Managers* Claude Miller & Roland Thénot, *Assistant Director* Suzanne Schiffman, *Source Report on Victor from the Aveyron* (1806) Jean Itard, *Script* François Truffaut & Jean Gruault, *Camera* Nestor Almendros with Philippe Théaudière, *Music* Vivaldi, *Editor* Agnès Guillemot with Yann Dedet, *Continuity* Christine Pellé, *Sound* René Levert, *Art Direction* Jean Mandaroux, B&W, 83 minutes.
Cast: François Truffaut (Dr Itard), Jean-Pierre Cargol (Victor), Françoise Seigner (Mme Guérin), Jean Dasté (Dr Pinel).

L'Enfant sauvage is a near-documentary dealing with the true story of the education of a young boy found living wild in the Aveyron.

Domicile conjugal
(UK/USA: Bed and Board, 1970)
Crew: Director François Truffaut, **Executive Producer** Marcel Berbert, **Production Managers** Claude Miller & Roland Thénot, **Assistant Directors** Suzanne Schiffman & Jean-François Stévenin, **Script** François Truffaut, Claude de Givray & Bernard Revon, **Camera** Nestor Almendros, **Music** Antoine Duhamel, **Editors** Agnès Guillemot, Yann Dedet, Martine Kalfon, **Continuity** Christine Pellé, **Sound** René Levert, **Art Direction** Jean Mandaroux, Colour, 100 minutes.
Cast: Jean-Pierre Léaud (Antoine Doinel), Claude Jade (Christine), Hiroko Berghauer (Kyoko).
Domicile conjugal is the fourth film in the Doinel cycle. Antoine is now married and has a son and a Japanese mistress.

Les Deux Anglaises et le Continent
(UK: Anne and Muriel, USA: Two English Girls, 1971)
Crew: Director François Truffaut, Executive Producer Marcel Berbert, **Production Managers** Claude Miller & Roland Thénot, **Assistant Director** Suzanne Schiffman, **Novel** Henri-Pierre Roché, **Script** François Truffaut & Jean Gruault, **Camera** Nestor Almendros, **Music** Georges Delerue, **Editors** Yann Dedet & Martine Barraqué, **Continuity** Christine Pellé, **Sound** René Levert, **Art Direction** Michel de Broin, **Costumes** Gitt Magrini, Colour, 132 minutes.
Cast: Jean-Pierre Léaud (Claude Roc), Kika Markham (Anne Brown), Stacey Tendeter (Muriel Brown), Sylvia Marriott (Mrs Brown), Marie Mansart (Claire Roc), Philippe Léotard (Diurka),

Colour, 132 minutes.
In Les Deux Anglaises et le Continent two English girls fall in love with the same man, a French writer and aesthete.

Une belle fille comme moi
(UK: A Gorgeous Bird Like Me, USA: Such a Gorgeous Kid Like Me, 1972)
Crew: Director François Truffaut, **Executive Producer** Marcel Berbert, **Production Managers** Claude Miller & Roland Thénot, **Assistant Director** Suzanne Schiffman, **Novel** Such a Gorgeous Kid Like Me Henry Farrell, **Script** François Truffaut & Jean-Loup Dabadie, **Camera** Pierre-William Glenn & Walter Bal, **Music** Georges Delerue, **Editors** Yann Dedet & Martine Barraqué, **Continuity** Christine Pellé, **Sound** René

Levert, **Art Direction** Jean-Pierre Kohut-Svelko & Jean-François Stévenin, **Costumes** Monique Dury, Colour, 100 minutes.
Cast: Bernadette Lafont (Camille Bliss), André Dussolier (Stanislas Prévine), Philippe Léotard (Clovis Bliss), Guy Marchand (Sam Golden), Claude Brasseur (Maître Murène), Charles Denner (Arthur).
Une belle fille comme moi is a fast-paced comedy about an uninhibited young woman imprisoned for deceiving and murdering a series of lovers in pursuit of a singing career.

La Nuit américaine
(UK: Day for Night, 1973)
Crew: Director François Truffaut, **Executive Producer** Marcel Berbert, **Production Managers** Claude Miller, Roland Thénot & Alex Maineri, **Assistant Directors** Suzanne Schiffman & Jean-François Stévenin, **Script** François Truffaut, Jean-Louis Richard & Suzanne Schiffman, **Camera** Pierre-William Glenn & Walter Bal, **Editors** Yann Dedet & Martine Barraqué, **Continuity** Christine Pellé, **Sound** René Levert, Harrik Maury, **Music** Georges Delerue, **Art Direction** Damien Lanfranchi, Colour, 115 minutes.
Cast: François Truffaut (Ferrand), Nathalie Baye (Joëlle), Jean-Pierre Léaud (Alphonse), Jacqueline Bisset (Julie Baker), David Markham (Dr Nelson), Nike Arrighi (Odile), Valentina Cortese (Séverine), Dani (Liliane), Alexandra Stewart (Stacey).
La Nuit américaine shows the highs and lows of making a film.

L'Histoire d'Adèle H.
(UK/USA: The Story of Adele H., 1975)
Crew: Director François Truffaut, **Executive Producer** Marcel Berbert, **Production Managers** Claude Miller, Roland Thénot & Patrick Miller, **Assistant Directors** Suzanne Schiffman & Carl

Hathwell, **Book** *The Diary of Adèle H.* ed. Frances Guille, **Script** François Truffaut, Jean Gruault with Frances Guille, **Camera** Nestor Almendros, **Music** Maurice Jaubert, **Editors** Yann Dedet & Martine Barraqué, **Continuity** Christine Pellé, **Sound** Jean-Pierre Ruh & Michel Laurent, **Art Direction** Jean-Pierre Kohut-Svelko, Colour, 95 minutes.
Cast: Isabelle Adjani (Adèle Hugo), Bruce Robinson (Lieutenant Pinson), Sylvia Marriott (Mrs Saunders), Joseph Blatchley (Bookshop owner), François Truffaut (Officer).
L'Histoire d'Adèle H. is a biographical film about the obsessive love of Victor Hugo's daughter for an English officer.

L'Argent de poche
(UK/USA: Small Change, 1976)
Crew: Director François Truffaut, **Executive Producer** Marcel Berbert, **Production Managers** Roland Thénot & Daniel Messere, **Assistant Directors** Suzanne Schiffman & Alain Maline, **Script** François Truffaut & Suzanne Schiffman, **Camera** Pierre-William Glenn with Jean-François Gondre, Florent Bazin & Jean-Claude Vicquery, **Music** Maurice Jaubert, **Editors** Yann Dedet & Martine Barraqué, **Continuity** Christine Pellé with Laura Truffaut, **Sound** Michel Laurent & Michel Brethey, **Art Direction** Jean-Pierre Kohut-Svelko, Colour, 105 minutes.
Cast: Jean-François Stévenin (Jean-François Richet), Virginie Thévenet (Lydie Richet), Nicole Félix (mother of Grégory), Francis Devlaeminck (M Riffle), Tania Torrens (Mme Riffle), Éva Truffaut (Patricia), Laura Truffaut (Madeleine Doinel).
L'Argent de poche is a film about childhood and early adolescence, set in a boys' school in provincial France.

L'Homme qui aimait les femmes
(UK/USA: The Man Who Loved Women, 1977)
Crew: Director François Truffaut, **Executive Producer** Marcel Berbert, **Production Managers** Roland Thénot with Philippe Lièvre & Lydie Mahias, **Assistant Directors** Suzanne Schiffman &

Alain Maline, **Camera** Nestor Almendros with Anne Trigaux & Florent Bazin, **Music** Maurice Jaubert, **Editor** Martine Barraqué, **Continuity** Christine Pellé, **Sound** Michel Laurent & Jean Fontaine, **Art Direction** Jean-Pierre Kohut-Svelko, Pierre Compertz & Jean-Louis Povéda, Colour, 118 minutes.
Cast: Charles Denner (Bertrand Morane), Brigitte Fossey (Geneviève Bigey), Nelly Borgeaud (Delphine Grezel), Nathalie Baye (Martine Desdoits), Leslie Caron (Véra), Geneviève Fontanel (Hélène).
L'Homme qui aimait les femmes is a comedy relating the story of Bertrand Morane, serial womaniser.

La Chambre verte
(UK/USA: The Green Room, 1978)
Crew: Director François Truffaut, **Executive Producer** Marcel Berbert, **Production Managers** Roland Thénot & Geneviève Lefebvre, **Assistant Directors** Suzanne Schiffman & Emmanuel Clot, **Short Stories** *The Altar of the Dead*, *The Beast in the Jungle*, *Friends of Friends* Henry James, **Script** François Truffaut & Jean Gruault, **Camera** Nestor Almendros with Anne Trigaux & Florent Bazin, **Music** Maurice Jaubert, **Editor** Martine Barraqué, **Continuity** Christine Pellé, **Sound** Michel Laurent & Jean-Louis Ugnetto, **Art Direction** Jean-Pierre Kohut-Svelko, Pierre Compertz & Jean-Louis Povéda, Colour, 94 minutes.

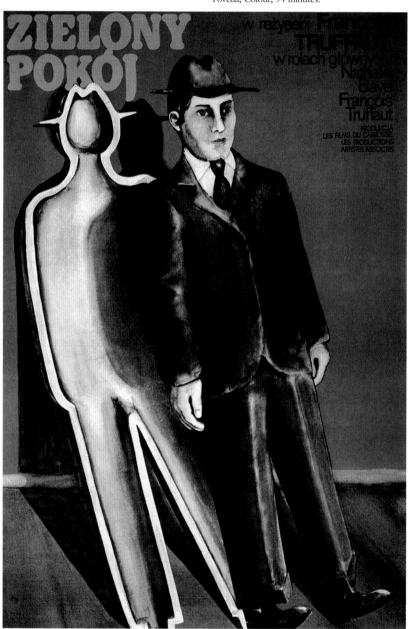

Cast: François Truffaut (Julien Davenne), Nathalie Baye (Cécilia Mandel), Jean Dasté (Bernard Humbert), Jane Lobre (Mme Rambaud).
La Chambre verte deals with loss and grief, recounting the story of Julien Davenne's obsessive love for his deceased wife.

L'Amour en fuite

(UK/USA: Love on the Run, 1979)
Crew: *Director* François Truffaut, *Executive Producer* Marcel Berbert, *Production Manager* Roland Thénot, *Assistant Directors* Suzanne Schiffman, Emmanuel Clot & Nathalie Seaver, *Script* François Truffaut, Suzanne Schiffman, Jean

Aurel & Marie-France Pisier, *Camera* Nestor Almendros with Florent Bazin & Emilia-Pakull-Latorre, *Music* Georges Delerue, *Editor* Martine Barraqué, *Continuity* Christine Pellé, *Sound* Michel Laurent, *Art Direction* Jean-Pierre Kohut-Svelko, Pierre Compertz & Jean-Louis Povéda, Colour, 94 minutes.
Cast: Jean-Pierre Léaud (Antoine Doinel), Claude Jade (Christine), Marie-France Pisier (Colette), Dani (Liliane), Dorothée (Sabine), Daniel Mesguich (Xavier Barnérias), Julien Bertheau (M Lucien).
L'Amour en fuite, last in the Doinel series, finds Antoine in the throes of divorce, writing a second autobiography and falling for Sabine.

Le Dernier Métro

(UK/USA: The Last Metro, 1980)
Crew: *Director* François Truffaut, *Executive Producer* Jean-José Richer, *Production Managers* Roland Thénot & Jean-Louis Godroy, *Assistant Directors* Suzanne Schiffman & Emmanuel Clot, *Script* François Truffaut, Suzanne Schiffman & Jean-Claude Grumberg, *Camera* Nestor Almendros with Florent Bazin, Emilia-Pakull-Latorre & Tessa Racine, *Music* Georges Delerue,

Editors Martine Barraqué, Marie-Aimée Debril & Jean-François Giré, *Continuity* Christine Pellé, *Sound* Michel Laurent Michel Mellier & Daniel Couteau, *Art Direction* Jean-Pierre Kohut-Svelko, Pierre Compertz, Jean-Louis Povéda & Roland Jacob, Colour, 128 minutes.
Cast: Catherine Deneuve (Marion Steiner), Heinz Bennent (Lucas Steiner), Gérard Depardieu (Bernard Granger), Jean Poiret (Jean-Loup Cottins), Jean-Louis Richard (Daxiat), Sabine Haudepin (Nadine Marsac).
Le Dernier Métro is set during the German Occupation and deals with the life and loves of a group of people who work in a Paris theatre.

La Femme d'à côté

(UK/USA: The Woman Next Door, 1981)
Crew: *Director* François Truffaut, *Executive Producer* Armand Barbault, *Production Managers* Roland Thénot with Jacques Vidal & Françoise Héberlé, *Assistant Directors* Suzanne Schiffman, Alain Tasma & Gilles Loutfi, *Script* François Truffaut, Suzanne Schiffman & Jean Aurel, *Camera* William Lubtchansky with Caroline Champetier & Barcha Bauer, *Music* Georges Delerue, *Editors* Martine Barraqué, Marie-Aimée Debril & Catherine Dryzmalkowski, *Continuity* Christien Pellé, *Sound* Michel Laurent, Michel Mellier, Jacques Maumont & Daniel Couteau, *Art Direction* Jean-Pierre Kohut-Svelko, Pierre Compertz & Jacques Peisach, Colour, 106 minutes.
Cast: Gérard Depardieu (Bernard Coudray), Fanny Ardant (Mathilde Bauchard), Henri Garcin (Philippe Bauchard), Michèle Baumgartner (Arlette Coudray), Véronique Silver (Odile Jouve), Roger van Hool (Roland Duguet).
La Femme d'à côté is the tragic story of a love that is out of control.

Vivement dimanche!

(UK: Finally Sunday!, USA: Confidentially Yours!, 1983)
Crew: *Director* François Truffaut, *Executive Producer* Armand Barbault, *Production Managers* Roland Thénot & Jacques Vidal, *Assistant Directors* Suzanne Schiffman, Rosine Robiolle & Pascal Deux, *Novel The Long Saturday Night* Charles Williams, *Script* François Truffaut, Suzanne Schiffman & Jean Aurel, *Camera* Nestor Almendros with Florent Bazin & Tessa Racine, *Music* Georges Delerue, *Editors* Martine Barraqué, Marie-Aimée Debril & Colette Achouche, *Continuity* Christine Pellé, *Sound* Pierre Gamet, Jacques Maumont, Bernard Chaumeil & Daniel Couteau, *Art Direction* Hilton McConnico, B&W, 111 minutes.
Cast: Jean-Louis Trintignant (Julien Vercel), Caroline Sihol (Marie-Christine Vercel), Fanny Ardant (Barbara Becker), Philippe Laudenbach (M Clément), Philippe Morier-Genoud (Superintendent Santinelli), Jean-Louis Richard (Louison).
Vivement dimanche! is a Hollywood-style comedy thriller. An estate agent, falsely accused of murder, is rescued by his resourceful and beautiful secretary.

Bibliography

Bibliography
- **Waltz, Eugene P.:** *François Truffaut, A Guide to References and Resources.* G. K. Hall and Co. 1982

Books by Truffaut
- *Le Cinéma selon Hitchcock* (with Helen Scott). Robert Laffont 1966. New edition revised and enlarged published as Hitchcock/Truffaut. Ramsay 1984, (trans.) Simon and Shuster 1984, Gallimard 1993
- *Les Aventures d'Antoine Doinel.* Mercure de France 1970. New edition Ramsay Poche Cinéma 1987
- *L'Enfant sauvage.* Editions G.P. 1970
- *La Nuit américaine and Journal de Fahrenheit 451.* Seghers 1974
- *Les Films de ma vie.* Flammarion 1975
- *The Films in My Life*, translated by Leonard Mayhew. Simon & Schuster 1978
- *L'Argent de poche, Cinéroman.* Flammarion, Paris, 1976
- *L'Homme qui aimait les femmes, Cinéroman.* Flammarion 1977
- *Truffaut par Truffaut.* Rabourdin, Dominique (ed.), Editions Du Chêne 1985
- *Truffaut by Truffaut.* Rabourdin, Dominique (ed.), translated by Robert Erich Wolf, Harry N. Abrams 1987
- *Le Plaisir des yeux.* Flammarion 1987
- *Les Mistons.* Editions Ciné Sud 1987
- *La Petite Voleuse.* Editions Christian Bourgois 1988
- *François Truffaut Correspondance.* Jacob, G. and de Givray, C. (eds.), 5 Continents Hatier 1988; Livre de poche 1993
- *François Truffaut Letters.* Jacob, G. and de Givray, C. (eds.), translated by Gilbert Adair, Faber & Faber 1989
- *Jules et Jim.* Editions du Seuil 1995

Books on Truffaut and his films
- **Allen, Don:** *Finally Truffaut.* Secker and Warburg 1985
- **Auzel, Dominique:** *Truffaut. Les Mille et Une Nuits américaines.* Henri Veyrier 1990
- **Bastide, Bernard:** *François Truffaut, Les Mistons.* Ciné-Sud 1987
- **Bonnafons, Elizabeth:** *François Truffaut, L'Age d'homme.* 1981
- **Braudy, Leo (ed.):** *Focus on Shoot the Piano Player.* Prentice-Hall 1972
- **Collet, Jean:** *Le Cinéma de François Truffaut.* Lherminier 1977
- **Collet, Jean:** *François Truffaut.* Lherminier 1985
- **Dalmais, Hervé:** *Truffaut.* Rivages Cinéma 1987
- **Desjardins, Aline:** *Aline Desjardins s'entretient avec François Truffaut.* Ramsay 1987
- **Dixon, Wheeler Winston:** *The Early Film Criticism of François Truffaut.* Indiana University Press 1993
- **Fanne, Dominique:** *L'Univers de François Truffaut.* Le Cerf 1972
- **Fischer, Robert (ed.):** *Monsieur Truffaut, wie haben Sie das gemacht?* Wilhelm Heyne 1993
- **Fischer, Robert:** *Vivement Truffaut!* CICIM, no. 41, November 1994
- *François Truffaut. Cinématographe*, no. 105 December 1984
- **Gillain, Anne:** *Le Cinéma selon François Truffaut.* Flammarion 1988
- **Gillain, Anne:** *François Truffaut, le secret perdu.* Hatier 1991
- **Guérif, François:** *François Truffaut.* Edilig 1988
- **Holmes, Diana and Ingram, Robert:** *François Truffaut.* Manchester University Press 1998
- **Insdorf, Annette:** *François Truffaut.* Boston, Twayne Publishers 1978; Cambridge University Press 1994
- **Insdorf, Annette:** *François Truffaut, Le cinéma est-il magique?* Ramsay 1989
- **Insdorf, Annette:** *François Truffaut.* Collection 'Découvertes' Gallimard 1996
- **Le Berre, Carole:** *François Truffaut.* Cahiers du cinéma 1993
- **Nicholls, David:** *François Truffaut.* B.T. Batsford 1993
- **Petrie, Graham:** *The Cinema of François Truffaut.* A.S. Barnes/A. Zwemmer 1970
- **Monaco, James:** *The New Wave.* Oxford University Press 1976
- **Simondi, Mario (ed.):** *François Truffaut.* La Casa Usher 1982
- *Le Roman de François Truffaut. Cahiers du cinéma,* special edition, December 1984

Biographies
- **Cahoreau, Gilles:** *François Truffaut 1932–84.* Julliard 1989
- **De Baecque, Antoine and Toubiana, Serge:** *François Truffaut.* Gallimard 1996, Alfred A. Knopf 1999

Websites
- www.imdb.com
- iihm.imag.fr/truffaut/

Notes

1. **Gide, André:** *Si le grain ne meurt.* Gallimard, 1955 edition. Pg. 245.
2. **Holmes, Diana and Ingram, Robert:** *François Truffaut.* Manchester University Press, 1998. Pg. 11.
3. *Le Roman de François Truffaut. Cahiers du cinéma,* December 1984. Pg. 54.
4. **Truffaut, François:** *Le Plaisir des yeux.* Flammarion, 1987. Pg. 40.
5. **Desjardins, Aline:** *Aline Desjardins s'entretient avec François Truffaut.* Ramsay 1987. Pg. 42
6. **Gillain, Anne:** *Le Cinéma selon François Truffaut.* Flammarion, 1988. Pg. 356.
7. **Insdorf, Annette:** *François Truffaut.* Cambridge University Press, 1994.
8. See note 3. Pg. 58.
9. Ibid. Pg. 49.
10. See note 6. Pg. 154.
11. **De Baecque, Antoine and Toubiana, Serge:** *François Truffaut.* Gallimard, 1996. Pg. 450.
12. See note 3. Pg. 48.
13. See note 2. Pg. 27.
14. See note 11. Pg. 395.
15. **Gillain, Anne:** *François Truffaut, Le Secret perdu.* Hatier, 1991. Pg. ii.
16. Ibid.
17. Ibid.
18. See note 3. Pg. 115.
19. Ibid. Pg. 135.
20. **Bastide, Bernard:** *François Truffaut, Les Mistons.* Ciné-Sud 1987. Pg. 10.
21. See note 11. Pg. 21.
22. See note 5. Pg. 12.
23. **Truffaut, François:** 'Une certaine tendance du cinéma français.' *Cahiers du cinéma,* January 1954.
24. See note 3. Pg. 73.
25. See note 2. Pg. 25.
26. See note 5. Pg. 29.
27. See note 3. Pg.10.
28. See note 11. Pgs. 131–132.
29. See note 6. Pg. 357.
30. See note 4. Pg. 23.
31. Ibid. Pg. 25.
32. Ibid. Pg. 40.
33. Ibid. Pg. 37.
34. See note 6. Pg. 129.
35. **Jacob, Gilles and de Givray, Claude (eds.):** *François Truffaut Correspondance.* 5 Continents Hatier, 1988. Pg. 172.
36. See note 6. Pg. 129.
37. Ibid.
38. Ibid. Pg. 138.
39. See note 2. Pgs. 59–77.
40. See note 15. Pg. 11
41. See note 35. Pg. 202.
42. See note 5. Pg. 51.
43. See note 6. Pg. 154.
44. Ibid. Pg. 173.
45. Ibid. Pg. 179.
46. Ibid.
47. Ibid. Pg. 405.
48. See note 11. Pg. 326.
49. See note 6. Pg. 192.
50. Ibid. Pg. 204.
51. Ibid. Pg. 205.
52. See note 3. Pg. 113.
53. See note 11. Pg. 402.
54. Ibid. Pg. 361.
55. See note 5. Pg. 59.
56. See note 6. Pg. 397.
57. Ibid. Pg. 248.
58. Ibid. Pg. 201.
59. See note 4. Pg. 39.
60. See note 6. Pg. 334.
61. Ibid. Pg. 282.
62. Ibid. Pg. 280.
63. Ibid. Pg. 261.
64. See note 11. Pg. 430.
65. See note 6. Pg. 296.
66. Ibid. Pg. 299.
67. Ibid. Pg. 301.
68. See note 4. Pg. 183.
69. See note 2. Pg. 151.
70. See note 6. Pg. 331.
71. Ibid. Pg. 375.
72. See note 3. Pg. 107.
73. See note 6. Pg. 342.
74. See note 11. Pg. 478.
75. See note 5. Pg. 54.
76. See note 4. Pg. 27.
77. See note 6. Pg. 356.
78. See note 2. Pg. 131.
79. See note 6. Pg. 360.
80. Ibid. Pg. 369.
81. Ibid. Pg. 373.
82. Ibid. Pg. 375.
83. Ibid. Pg. 197.
84. See note 4. Pg. 201.
85. See note 6. Pgs. 383-384.
86. **Rabourdin, Dominique (ed.):** *Truffaut by Truffaut.* Harry N. Abrams 1987. Pg. 171.
87. See note 4. Pg. 16.
88. See note 6. Pg. 392.
89. See note 2. Pgs. 194–196.
90. See note 35. Pg. 588.
91. See note 6. Pg. 329.
92. See note 2. Pg. 141.
93. See note 4. Pgs. 184–185.
94. See note 11. Pg. 544.
95. See note 6. Pg. 417.
96. Ibid. Pg. 419.
97. See note 3. Pg. 106.
98. See note 6. Pg. 421.
99. See note 11. Pg. 560.